Orion
An Epic English Poem

Edited by
Andrew Barger

Also Edited by Andrew Barger
**Edgar Allan Poe
Annotated and Illustrated
Entire Stories and Poems**

Fiction by Andrew Barger
Coffee with Poe

AndrewBarger.com

Bottletree Books LLC

BottletreeBooks.com

Orion
An Epic English Poem

**Edited by
Andrew Barger**

First Edition
Manufactured in the United States or the United Kingdom
ISBN: 978-1-933747-09-5

Printed on 100% recycled paper in both
the United States and United Kingdom
(20% Post Consumer Waste)

Font: Bookman Old Style

Copyrights: © Copyright Andrew Barger 2008. All rights reserved. Registered at the U.S. Copyright Office under Reg. No. TXu001572062. No part of this publication may be reproduced in any way or by any means electronic, mechanical, photocopying, recording, or stored in an information retrieval system of any kind, without the prior written permission of Andrew Barger, except in the case of brief quotations embodied in reviews and scholarly articles. Digital images of the front and back covers may be resized and shown as "fair use" for purposes of selling and promoting the book. Copyright exists in the selection, coordination and arrangement of the footnotes, background information, and images within, both individually and collectively. Please respect the copyrights.

Trademarks: BOTTLETREE, BOTTLETREE BOOKS, Bottletree Logo, and related trade dress, including all cover art designs are the trademarks/trade dress of Bottletree Books, LLC, and may not be used without written permission, except digital images of the front and back covers may be resized and shown as "fair use" for purposes of selling and promoting the book.

BottletreeBooks.com

CONTENTS

List of Illustrations

Illustrations 5

Introduction by Andrew Barger

Rescuing "Orion" 6

Biography by Edward Cornelius Towne

Richard Henry (Hengist) Horne: Short Biography 10

Epic Poem

"Orion: An Epic English Poem" 15

Afterword by Richard Henry (Hengist) Horne

Afterword 114

Review by Edgar Allan Poe

Review of "Orion: An Epic Poem in Three Books" 120

Illustrations

Richard Horne. 10, 114

Artemis 23

Zeus 33

Orion 42

Hephaestus 53

Pan 75

Poseidon 88

Rescuing "Orion"

Before you is a classic English poem written in allegory style. Its *overtones* consist of aesthetically pleasing writing for epic poetry with an inescapable Shakespearian tinge. It is pinned to classical Greek mythology of superior deities. "Orion's" *undertones* tell us to eschew brute force for that of the higher mind. This ship of enlightenment had enough steam behind it in 1843 to be published in ten new editions well into the Nineteenth Century and was the crowning achievement of its English author, Richard Henry Horne. Sadly, however, "Orion" has been out of print for eighty years.

Occasionally great literary ships lose their bearings and are lost at sea. In dark storms they fall out of publication and circulation among intelligent readers. Thankfully the digital age of books is upon us and because of it electronic versions of great works will never die by fire as those befalling titles in the Library of Alexandria; and more recently those burned in the Cotton Library on the grounds of the Ashburnham House in 1731. Today we can only surmise as to the tragedies of Æschylus and Homer's son; the original text of the Greek "Chronicon," and the lost orations of Isæus and Lysias. Because "Orion" has been out of print for eighty years, the vast population, even many schooled in Nineteenth Century English literature, are unaware of the epic poem's existence. As stated in Canto the Third of "Orion": *Ignorance chokes us, and time outwits us.*

The epic poem before you was last published in 1928 by Scholartis Press of London. When England's Great Depression ensued three years later, Scholartis Press closed its doors and access to this necessary poem for every person of literature was nearly smashed against the rocky outcroppings of obscurity. This most surely would have been the case if not for a shining lighthouse by the name of Edgar Allan Poe. In 1843 Richard Henry (Hengist) Horne set the literary world ablaze by publishing his *magnum opus*. The fire soon spread to America, helped in large part by a gushing review of the poem by Poe in *Graham's Magazine* during March of 1844.

This glowing and poignant review is appended after the poem to give pointed insight into the epic as well as Poe's philosophy on poetry. I came upon it while researching material for a recent book I edited titled: "Edgar Allan Poe: Annotated and Illustrated Entire Stories and Poems." Thanks to Poe's beacon in the night, "Orion," this giant tanker of a poem, did not end its life in a watery grave. It has merely been lost at sea. On this 165th anniversary of its original publication let's guide it back to shore.

I. The Accessible "Orion"
Here "Orion" is brought to life as never before with annotations, background into the life of Richard Horne, illustrations, photos, and a review by arguably one of America's greatest poets and critics, Edgar Allan Poe. He was a champion for the poem's cause in America.

II. Annotations/Definitions/Translations
The text before you is the Australian Edition of "Orion: An Epic Poem in Three Books" published by James J. Blundell & Co. in 1874. To enhance its readability, troublesome words and turns of phrase are defined. This prevents one from having to leave the meter of the poem while experiencing it. Having to consult a reference book while reading "Orion" is akin to stopping an orchestra because one has to research the key being played.

III. Illustrations
Throughout "Orion" you will find various illustrations of classical Greek mythological characters. Like the Biblical Goliath, every giant has a weakness and "Orion" is no different. The flaw here comes from the classical names Horne used in the epic poem, which as you'll see from his Afterword, he did not mean to conjure the classical notions of trait and personality associated with these mythical characters. If a poet names his characters classical names it is inevitable that their historical baggage will be dragged along by readers perusing the text. If a poet does make this mistake in the first edition, by all means change it in the subsequent nine editions. Unfortunately, this is not the case and the giant "Orion" has its exposed flaw right in the center of its forehead, open to a stone flung by the sling of David (or Edgar Allan Poe).

IV. Poem Line Breaks
"Orion" is not written in the normal rhyming lines and cadenced meter of traditional poetry. You will, however, find that various intonations and resonance exists among the verses. The

quatrains are best read as long paragraphs and run-on sentences. The published form of this epic poem in the Nineteenth Century consisted of a book that was only five inches across. Hence the often awkward line breaks in the text of the poem. Regardless, the original format has been kept.

V. Afterword by Horne

The Afterword is actually a *Foreword* written by Richard Horne in the Australian edition of "Orion," published in 1854. In the various reprints of "Orion" the author penned different variants of the Foreword with the one you have before you the most revealing.

VI. Poe's Review

The Edgar Allan Poe review you have at the end of this book is from *Graham's Magazine*, March of 1844. Two years later segments of the poem were later included by Rufus Griswold in the third edition of "The Poets and Poetry of England, in the Nineteenth Century." Poe was known to write with an iron pen and was one of the Nineteenth Century's harshest critics of suspect literary efforts. When his review of "Orion," included the following praise, the literary world took note.

> It is our deliberate opinion that, in all that regards the loftiest and holiest attributes of the true Poetry, "Orion" has *never* been excelled. Indeed we feel strongly inclined to say that it has never been *equaled*.
>
> .
> .
>
> The description of the Hell in "Paradise Lost" is *altogether inferior* in graphic effect, in originality, in expression, in the true imagination — to these magnificent — to these unparalleled passages.
>
> .
> .
>
> "Orion" will be admitted, by every man of genius, to be one of the noblest, if not the very noblest poetical work of the age. Its defects are trivial and conventional — its beauties intrinsic and *supreme*.

At publication of his review, Poe had yet to publish "The Raven," "Annabel Lee," "The Bells," or "Ulalume," four of his best poems;

yet he had already published such classics as "The Conqueror Worm," "To Helen," "The Doomed City," and "The Haunted Palace." Poe gets all the credit for rescuing this poem. He is the beacon in the night.

In the ensuing pages you will find "Orion" saved from the waves of literary obscurity. It deserves a place next to "Beowulf," our oldest surviving epic poem in the English language. It is one of the ancient poem's offsprings from England; a poetic progeny so to speak, with strong Shakespearean influences along with those of the ancient Greeks. It can only be hoped that its excellent prose and storyline will serve to spawn more epic poetry for the artistic enjoyment of all. You will find yourself returning to it. "Orion" is that good of a poem. As Charlotte Brontë stated in her letter to Richard Horne on December 15, 1847, and collected in "Charlotte Brontë and Her Circle," Clement King Shorter, 1986, p. 434:

> . . . there are passages I shall recur to again and yet again – passages instinct both with power and beauty. All through it is genuine – pure from one flaw of affection, rich in noble imagery.

One-hundred twenty-four years—to the day—after the death of Richard Horne, I once again give you "Orion: An Epic Poem in Three Books."

Andrew Barger

Andrew Barger
March 13, 2008

Richard Henry (Hengist) Horne
A Short Biography

"Library of the World's Best Literature, Ancient and Modern," Edward Cornelius Towne, Vol. XIII, 1897, p. 7641.

Richard Horne

"Literary Anecdotes of the Nineteenth Century: Contributions Towards a Literary History of the Period," William Robertson Nicoll and Thomas J. Wise, 1895, p. 237.

RICHARD HENRY HENGIST HORNE (1803-1884), English poet and essayist, author of more than twenty volumes of verse and prose, is now chiefly remembered for his epic poem and large editions of it he published at a farthing a copy, "to show his appreciation of the low esteem into which heroic poetry had fallen." The fourth edition commanded a shilling, and the fifth a half-crown. Ten editions had been exhausted by 1874.

Home's life was adventurous and interesting. He was born in London January 1st, 1803, was educated at Sandhurst, and entered as midshipman the Mexican navy, where he served till the close of the War of Independence. He then returned to London to begin a literary career. To his early period belong two tragedies, "Cosmo de' Medici" and contain fine passages. A poem sent to him for criticism by Elizabeth Barrett Browning opened the way to a cordial friendship and a correspondence of seven years. These delightful letters were published in 1877. Mrs. Browning contributed to Home's "Poems of Geoffrey Chaucer Modernized," and wrote several essays for his a collection of criticisms published in 1844.

In 1852 Home removed to Australia, and remained there until 1866; his book of this residence. Again returning to England, he continued literary work until his death at Margate, March 13th, 1884. His last works were tragedies, including curious prose tract, "Sithron the Star-Stricken" (1883), which he pretended to take from the Arabian. Poe said that his "Orion" might be called "a homily against supineness and apathy in the cause of human progress, and in favor of energetic action for the good of the race.... It is our deliberate opinion," he affirmed, "that in all that regards the loftiest and holiest attributes of true poetry, 'Orion' has never been excelled."

Orion

—

Book I

Book I

Canto the First

YE rocky heights of Chios,[1] where the snow,
Lit by the far-off and receding moon,
Now feels the soft dawn's purpling twilight creep
Over your ridges, while the mystic dews
Swarm down, and wait to be instinct with gold
And solar fire!—ye mountains waving brown
With thick-winged woods, and blotted with deep caves
In secret places; and ye paths that stray
E'en as ye list; what odours and what sighs
Tend your sweet silence through the star-showered night,
Like memories breathing of the Goddess forms
That left your haunts, yet with the day return!

And still more distant through the grey sky floats
The faint blue fragment of the dead moon's shell;
Not dead indeed, but vacant, since 'Tis now
Left by its bright Divinity. The snows
On steepest heights grave tints of dawn receive,
And mountains from the misty woodland rise
More clear of outline, while thick vapours curl
From off the valley streams, and spread away,
Till one by one the brooks and pools unveil
Their cold blue mirrors. From the great repose
What echoes now float on the listening air—
Now die away—and now again ascend,
Soft ringing from the valleys, caves, and groves,
Beyond the reddening heights? 'Tis Artemis[2] come
With all her buskined Nymphs[3] and sylvan rout,[4]
To scare the silence and the sacred shades,
And with dim music break their rapturous trance!

But soon the music swells, and as the gleam
Of sun-rise tips the summits tremblingly,
And the dense forests on their sides exchange
Shadows opaque for warm transparent tones,

---

[1] Fifth largest Greek Island (pronounced 'ky-as'), note the similarity to the word "chaos"
[2] Daughter of Zeus and Leto in Greek mythology; Equated with Diana, goddess of Roman mythology
[3] Female being in Greek myth that is relegated to a particular woodland or goddess such as Artemis
[4] Woodland haunt or withdrawl

Though still of depth and grandeur, nearer grows
The revelry; and echoes multiply
Behind the rocks and uplands, with the din[5]
Of reed-pipe, timbrel, and clear silver horns,
40   With cry of Wood-nymphs, Fauns,[6] and chasing hounds.

   Afar the hunt in vales below has sped,
But now behind the wooded mount ascends,
Threading its upward mazes of rough boughs,
45 Mossed trunks and thickets, still invisible,
Although its jocund[7] music fills the air
With cries and laughing echoes, mellowed all
By intervening woods and the deep hills.

50   The scene in front two sloping mountain sides
Displayed; in shadow one, and one in light.
The loftiest on its summit now sustained
The sun-beams, raying like a mighty wheel
Half seen, which left the forward surface dark
55 In its full breadth of shade; the coming sun
Hidden as yet behind: the other mount,
Slanting transverse, swept with an eastward face,
Catching the golden light. Now, while the peal
Of the ascending chase told that the rout
60 Still midway rent the thickets, suddenly
Along the broad and sunny slope appeared
he shadow of a stag[8] that fled across,
Followed by a Giant's shadow with a spear!

65   Hunter of Shadows, thou thyself a Shade,
Be comforted in this,—that substance holds
No higher attributes; one sovran[9] law
Alike develops both, and each shall hunt
Its proper object, each in turn commanding
70 The primal impulse, till gaunt Time become
A shadow cast on space, to fluctuate,
Waiting the breath of the Creative Power
To give new types for substance yet unknown:

---

[5] Noise
[6] Horned creature with upper torso of a man and legs of a goat
[7] Merry
[8] Male deer
[9] Supreme

So from faint nebulae[10] bright worlds are born;
75 So worlds return to vapour. Dreams design
Most solid lasting things, and from the eye
That searches life, death evermore retreats.

Substance unseen, pure mythos,[11] or mirage,
80 The shadowy chase has vanished; round the swell
Of the near mountain sweeps a bounding stag—
Round whirls a god-like Giant close behind—
O'er a fallen trunk the stag with slippery hoofs
Stumbles—his sleek knees lightly touch the grass—
85 Upwards he springs—but in his forward leap,
The Giant's hand hath caught him fast beneath
One shoulder tuft, and lifted high in air,
Sustains! Now Phoibos's[12] chariot rising bursts
Over the summits with a circling blaze,
90 Gilding those frantic antlers, and the head
Of that so glorious Giant in his youth,
Who, as he turns, the form succinct beholds
Of Artemis,—her bow, with points drawn back,
A golden hue on her white rounded breast
95 Reflecting, while the arrow's ample barb
Gleams o'er her hand, and at his heart is aimed.

The Giant lowered his arm—away the stag
Breast forward plunged into a thicket near;
100 The Goddess paused, and dropt her arrow's point—
Raised it again—and then again relaxed
Her tension, and while slow the shaft came gliding
Over the centre of the bow, beside
Her hand, and gently drooped, so did the knee.
105 Of that heroic shape do reverence
Before the Goddess. Their clear eyes had ceased
To flash, and gazed with earnest softening light.

His stature, though colossal, scarcely seemed
110 Beyond the heroic mould, such symmetry
His form displayed; and in his countenance
A noble honesty and ardour beamed,
With child-like faith, unconscious of themselves,
And of the world, its vanities and guile.

---

[10] Clouds
[11] Pattern of faith or beliefs
[12] Sun god

115	Eyes of deep blue, large waves of chestnut locks, A forehead wide, and every feature strong, Yet without heaviness or angry line, Had he; and as he knelt, a trustful smile That dreads no consequence, and quite forgets
120	All danger, lightly played around his mouth. Meanwhile the Nymphs and all the sylvan troop, Like wave on wave when coloured by the clouds, Pell-mell come rolling round the mountain side, And crowd about the Goddess, who commands
125	The hunt to pause. At once the music stops— And all the hounds, with wistful looks, crouch down.
	"Young Giant of the woods," said Artemis, "The bow, that ne'er till now its glittering points
130	Bent back without recoil and whirring twang— That sound a shaft's flight, and that flight a death— For once to its quiescent[13] shape returns Unsated.[14] 'Midst these woodland vales and heights Seldom I rove, but from my train, have Nymphs
135	Permission sought full oft to lead the chase Among these echoes and these fleeting shades. Thee have they seen, as now, bounding beyond Their swiftest hounds to bear the stag away. As thou once more hadst surely done this morn,
140	But for my presence. Say, then, whence thou spring'st— Where dwell'st thou-how art called-and wherefore thus Dar'st thou the sports of these my Wood-nymphs mar?"
	"Goddess!" the Giant answered, "I am sprung
145	From the great Trident-bearer,[15] Who sustains And rocks the floating earth, and from the nymph— A huntress joying in the dreamy woods— Euryale.[16] Little I use to speak, Save to my kindred giants, who in caves
150	Amid yon forest dwell, beyond the rocks, Or to my Cyclop[17] friends; nor know I what words Best suit a Goddess's ear. I and the winds Do better hold our colloquies, when shadows,

---

[13] Quiet state of being
[14] Unsatisfied
[15] Poseidon, god of sea and earthquakes in Greek myth
[16] Mother of Orion
[17] Giant race with one eye in center of forehead in Greek myth

After long hunting, vanish from my sight
155 Into some field of gloom. I am called 'Orion,'[18]—
And for the sports I have so often marred,
'Twas for my own I did it, but without
A thought of whose the Nymphs, or least design
Of evil. Wherefore, Artemis, pardon me;
160 Or if again thou'dst bend thy bow, first let me
To great Poseidon offer up a prayer,
That his divine waves with absorbing arms
May take my body rather than dull earth."

    With attitude relaxed from queenly pride
165 To yet more queenly grace, the shaft she placed
Within her burnished quiver, and the bow
A Nymph unstrung, while with averted face—
As gazing down the woodland vista slopes,
Which oft her bright orb silvered through black shades
170 When midnight throbbed to silence—Artemis asked,
"And who are these thy brothers of the cave,
And why dost with the Cyclops hold consort?"

    "My wood-friends all of ancestry renowned,
Claim for their sires heros, or kings, or gods;
175 And two of them have seen the ways of men;"
Orion answered, while with uplifted breast,
Like a smooth wave o'ergilded by the morn,
High heaving ere it cast itself ashore,
Buoyant, elate, and massively erect,
180 He stood. "They are my kindred thus descended,
And, though not brothers, yet we recognize
A sort of brotherhood in this decree
Of fate, or Zeus,[19]—that nature filled our frames
With larger share of bodily elements
185 Than others mortal born. Seven giants we,
Of different minds, and destinies, and powers,
Yet glorified alike in corporeal[20] forms.
Few are my years, O Artemis! few my needs,
Though large my fancied wants, and small my knowledge

---

[18] Giant hunter of Greek myth, also constellation - Orion's belt consisting of three stars and his shoulders and feet being formed by a retangle of four stars
[19] Ruled from Mount Olympus over all other gods
[20] Body or physical forms

190   Save of one art. Earth's deep metallic veins
      Hephaestus[21] taught me to refine and forge
      To shapes that in my fancy I devised,
      For use or ornament. To the lame God
      Grateful I felt, nor knew what thanks to give;
195   But, ere a shadow-hunter I became—
      A dreamer of strange dreams by day and night—
      For him I built a palace underground,
      Of iron, black and rough as his own hands.
      Deep in the groaning disembowelled earth,
200   The tower-broad pillars and huge stanchions,[22]
      And slant supporting wedges I set up,
      By the Cyclops aided-at my voice
      Which through the metal fabric rang and pealed
      In orders echoing far, like thunder-dreams.
205   With arches, galleries, and domes all carved—
      So that great figures started from the roof
      And lofty coignes,[23] or sat and downward gazed
      On those who strode below and gazed above—
      I filled it; in the centre framed a hall:
210   Central in that, a throne; and for the light,
      Forged mighty hammers that should rise and fall
      On slanted rocks of granite and of flint.
      Worked by a torrent, for whose passage down
      A chasm I hewed. And here the God could take,
215   Midst showery sparks and swathes of broad gold fire,
      His lone repose, lulled by the sounds he loved;
      Or, casting back the hammer-heads till they choked
      The water's course, enjoy, if so he wished,
      Midnight tremendous, silence, and iron sleep."
220
        Thus in rough phrase, and with no other grace
      Than forthright truth, Orion told his tale;
      Then smiling looked around upon the Nymphs
      Till all their bright eyes glowed and turned aside;
225   And then he gazed down at the couchant[24] hounds,
      Whose eyes and ears grew interrogative,
      For well the fleet-heeled robber they all knew.

---

[21] God of artisans, including blacksmiths and sculptors
[22] Vertical support posts
[23] Keystone of a high arch
[24] Lying on stomach with raised head

    Now spake an Ocean-nymph with sea-green eyes:
230 "Goddess, he hath not told thee all; his skill
    And strength, unaided—singing as he wrought—
    Scooped out the bay of Zankle,[25] framed its port;
    Banked up the rampire[26] that forbids the surge
    To break o'er Sicily; and a temple built
235 To the sea deities." "I had forgot;"
    Orion said : "These things, long since were done."

    "Hunter, I pardon thee, and from my Nymphs
    All memory of late offence I take,
    As though they ne'er had seen thee:" Artemis said,
240 With a sweet voice and look. "Retire awhile,
    Ye sylvan troop, to yonder deep-mossed dell;
    And thou, Orion, henceforth in my train
    Thy station take." More had the Goddess said,
    But o'er the whiteness of a neck that ne'er
245 One tanned kiss from the ardent sun received,
    A soft suffusion came; and waiting not
    Reply, her silver sandals glanced i' the rays,
    As doth a lizard playing on a hill,
    And on the spot where she that instant stood,
250 Nought but the bent and quivering grass was seen.

    Above the isle of Chios, night by night,
    The clear moon lingered ever on her course,
    Covering the forest foliage, where it swept
    In its unbroken breadth along the slopes,
255 With placid silver; edging leaf and trunk
    Where gloom clung deep around; but chiefly sought
    With melancholy splendour to illume
    The dark-mouthed caverns where Orion lay
    Dreaming among his kinsmen. Ere the breath
260 Of Phoibos' steeds rose from the wakening sea,
    And long before the immortal wheel-spokes cast
    Their hazy apparition up the sky
    Behind the mountain peaks, pale Artemis left
    Her fainting orb,[27] and touched the loftiest snows
265 With feet as pure, and white, and crystal cold,

---

[25] Bay of Messina founded in 725 B.C. and called Zankle by early Greeks
[26] Fortification
[27] Celestial body such as the sun

In the sweet misty woodland to rejoin
Orion with her Nymphs. And he was blest
In her divine smile, and his life began
A new and higher period, nor the haunts
Of those his giant brethren sought he now,
But shunned them and their ways, and slept alone
Upon a verdant rock, while o'er him floated
The clear moon, causing music in his brain
Until the sky-lark rose. He felt'Twas love.

Artemis

"The Mythology of Greece and Rome: With Special Reference to Its Use,"
Otto Seemann, 1877, p. 50.

Book I

Canto the Second

M̲ɪ̲ᴅ̲s̲ᴛ̲ ponderous substance had Orion's life
Dawned, and his acts were massive as his form.
Those his companions of the forest owned
Like corporal forces, but their several minds
5 And aims were not as his. The Worker he,
The builder-up of things, and of himself:
His wood-friends were Rhexergon,[28] of descent
Royal, heroic—breaker-down of things—
A coaster, skilled in fishing and in ships;—
10 Autarces,[29] arch-backed like the forest boar,
Short-haired, harsh-voiced, of fierce and wayward will;—
Harpax,[30] with large loose mouth, and restless hand,
Son of the God of Folly by a maid
Who cursed him—and the child, an idiot else,
15 Grew keen, in rapine taking great delight;—
Forceful Biastor;[31]—smooth Encolyon,[32]
The son of Hermes,[33] yet in all things slow,
With sight oblique and forehead slanting high,
The dull retarder, chainer of the wheel;—
20 And Akinetos[34]—who, since first the dawn
Sat on his marble forehead, ne'er had gazed
Onward with purpose of activity,
Nor felled a tree, nor hollowed out a cave,
Nor built a roof, nor aided any work,
25 Nor heaved a sigh, nor cared for anything
Save contemplation of the eternal scheme—
The Great Unmoved—a giant much revered.

　　Forgotten by their sires[35] in other loves,
30 Here had they chiefly dwelt, and in these caves,
Save two, Encolyon and the Great Unmoved,
Who came from Ithaca.[36] The islanders
Had driven them thence; and this the idle cause.
The barren stony land had ne'er produced

---

[28] Destroyer of establishments → Revolution
[29] Unruly and untamed → Rebellion
[30] Claptrap → Undisciplined
[31] Brute force → Brashness
[32] Circumspect → Conservative
[33] Greek god of boundaries
[34] Laziness → Apathy
[35] Masters
[36] Greek island in Ionian Sea

35	Enough of grain for food; but by the skill
	Of their artificers in iron and brass,
	And by their herds of goats and cloud-woolled sheep,
	With other isles the Ithacans exchanged,
	And each was well supplied. Encolyon's brain
40	Some goddess—and 'Twas Discord, as results
	Made plain—one night inspired with sage alarms,
	And straight the King of Ithaca he sought,
	Imploring him, "if that he duly prized
	A heaven-blest crown and subjects all content,
45	To drive the ships, sent from the neighbouring isles,
	Forth from his port, or sink the grain they brought:
	Else would his people, over-fed, grow slothful,
	Rude, and importunate[37] with new conceits,
	And soon degenerating in their race,
50	Neglect their proper island, and their King.
	But, on its own resources nobly forced,
	Then would the stony Ithaca become
	Great in herself by self-dependent power."
55	To this the King gave ear, and on the shore
	He, with Encolyon, for an omen prayed;
	And soon along the horizontal line
	Rising, they saw a threatening rack of clouds,
	Black as the fleet from Aulis[38] 'gainst doomed Troy,—
60	In after-time well known. Encolyon cried
	"Behold propitious anger on the isle,
	For its wrong doings!" Wherefore all the grain
	From friendly islands they, with scorn, sent back.
	A famine soon in Ithaca spread wide,
65	And hungry people prowled about at night,
	Then clamoured, and took arms—their war-cry "bread!"
	Thus was the dormant evil of their hearts
	Attested, and the King his people knew,
	And bitterly their want of reverence felt.
70	
	Encolyon, in his stature tall confiding,
	Though Akinetos warned him not to move,
	Went gravely forth the rebel throngs to meet.
	The politic giant's staid demeanour awed
75	The angry mass at first, and with their eyes

---

[37] Annoying

[38] In Greek mythology, port where Greek Navy assembled before striking off against Troy

They seemed to listen, doubtful of their ears,
So puzzling was his speech. He to the King
And his chief heroes then discoursed apart,
Convincing them that all the wheels went well.
80 With head bent sideways from the light, he looked
Like to some statesman of consummate mind
Working an ancient problem; and then spake
In language critical, final, stolid, astute,
Concluding with affectionate appeal
85 To common sense, and all we hold most dear.
Keep down—put back—prevent! O Gods prevent!"
This was his famous saying. Now the King
Led out his patriot army—but ere long
The army hungered too—the King was slain—
90 Encolyon fled, and hid within a ship.

    Forthwith a crowd to Akinetos thronged,
Crying, "What say'st thou, giant who art wise?
What shall we do?" And Akinetos said,
95 "Great hunger is a single thing—one want:
Satisfy that, and strength will be acquired
To multiply desire—wants without end!
Therefore be patient: leave all else to fate."

100   The people, stubborn as their own dry rocks—
Enraged as the wild winds—to reason deaf—
And also wanting food—cursed his calm thought—
Cast stones upon him, and had surely slain
But that without resistance he bore all,
105 And without word; so they, being tired, relented,
And bore him to the ship, where, in the hold,
Encolyon lay at length with in-drawn breath.
To Chios sailed the ship. The Ithacans
Chose a new king, and traded with the isles.
110
    In this companionship Orion's bent
Of nature had not merged; his working spirit
Sought from the fallen trunks and rocks to frame
Rude image of his fancies, till at length
115 He won Hephastos's love, from whom he learnt
The god's own solid art. But this attained,
And proved by mastery, a restless dream
Dawned on his soul which he desired to shape,
Yet knew not how, nor saw its like around,
120 But vaguely felt at times, and thought he saw

```
           In shadows. Wherefore through the forest depths,
           Through vales and over hills, a hunter fleet
           He chased his unknown hopes; and when the stag
           Or goat, or ounce,[39] he overtook and seized,
125        Ever he set them free, and e'en the bear
           And raging boar his spear refrained to strike,
           Save by its shadow, as they roaring fled.
           The bodily thing became to him as nought
           When gained; nor satisfied with efforts passed.
130
              Now from a Goddess did he quickly learn
           The mystery of his mood, and saw how vain
           His early life had been, and felt new roots
           Quicken within him, branches new that sprang
135        Aloft, and with expanding energies
           Tingled, and for immortal fruit prepared.

              She met him in her beauty. Oft when dawn
           With a grave red looked through the ash-pale woods,
140        And quick dews singing fell, while with a pulse
           As quick, Orion stood beneath the trees,
           And gazed upon the uncertain scene,—his heart
           Forewarned his senses with a rapturous thrill.
           He turned, and from the misty green afar,
145        In silence did the Goddess' train appear
           Bounding a thicket. Slow the crowding hounds
           Tript circling onward; Nymphs with quivered backs,
           And clear elastic limbs of nut-brown hue,
           Or like tanned wall-fruit, ripening and compact;
150        And short-horned Fauns down gazing on their pipes;
           And Oceanides[40] with tresses green
           Plaited in order, or by golden nets
           In various device confined, each bearing
           Shell lyres[41] and pearl-mouthed trumpets of the sea;
155        Dryads[42] and Oreads[43] decked with oak-leaf crowns
           And heath-bells, dancing in the fragrant air;
           And Sylvans, who, half Faun, half shepherd, lead
           A grassy life, with cymbals in each hand Pressed cross-
```

---

[39] Snow Leopard
[40] 3000 Nymphs that rule over all fresh water in Greek mythology
[41] U-shaped, stringed musical instrument played by Greeks when reciting
[42] Tree nymphs
[43] Mountain and valley nymphs

      wise on the breast, waiting the sign;—
160 Attendant round a pale gold chariot moved:
By two large-antlered milk-white stags 'Twas drawn,
Their sleek hides 'neath the fiue[44] dews quivering,
In delicate delight. Above them rose
The fair-haired Goddess, onward softly gliding,
165 As though erect she stood on wafted clouds.
She smiled not; but the crescent on her brow
Gleamed with a tender light. He knew 'Twas love.

      Giddy with happiness Orion's spirit
170 Now danced in air; his heart tumultous beat
Too high a measure and too wild, to taste
The fulness that he dreamed encompassed him,
But he could not encompass, nor scarce dare
Clearly to recognize. And Artemis smiled
175 Upon him with a radiance silver sweet,
And o'er his forehead oft her hand she waved,
Till visions of the purity of love
Above him floated, and his being filled.

180   Language of Gods she taught him; and pourtrayed;
But chief of all, in accents nobly sad,
She told of kindness by Poseidon done,
His ocean sire, when swan-necked Leto[45] bearing
Twins of bright destiny and heirs of heaven—
185 Herself and Phoibos—cruelly was driven
Through the bleak ways of earth, and found no rest,
Pursued by serpent jealousy, for Zeus
Had loved fair Leto; how Orion's sire
A floating isle that sometimes 'neath the waves
190 Drifted unseen, sometimes showed watery rocks,
Smote with his trident, and, majestical,
Delos[46] arose—stood fast—and gave a home
To fainting Leto,—and a place of birth
For deities—the Sun, and his loved Orb.
195 The mysteries, worship, and the sacrifice

---

[44] Tree with a small trunk that grows about 30 feet high at mature growth
[45] Daughter of Coeus and Phoebe in Greek mythology, Zeus fathered her twins: Apollo (Phoibos) and Artemis
[46] Greek island on which a temple was built to Apollo and to which Apollo and his mother Leto fled

Of her Ephesian Temple,[47] she displayed
Before his wondering thought, and oft he kenlt
In solitude, when of its hundred columns,
Each reared by kingly hands, wakeful he dreamed,
And felt his Goddess love too high removed.
The ocean realm below, and all its caves
And bristling vegetation, plant and flower,
And forests in their dense petrific[48] shade
Where the tides moan for sleep which never comes; All
this she taught him, and continually
Knowledge of human life made clear to him
Through facts and fables. He the intricate web
Of nature, gradually of himself began
To unwind, and see that gods and men were one—
Born of one element, imperfect both,
Yet aspirant, and with perfection's germ
Somewhere within. He brooded o'er these things.

One day, at noontide, when the chase was done,
Which with unresting speed since dawn had held,
The woods were all with golden fire alive,
And heavy limbs tingled with glowing heat.
Sylvans and Fauns at full length cast them down,
And cooled their flame-red faces in the grass,
Or o'er a streamlet bent, and dipped their heads
Deep as the top hair of their pointed ears;
While Nymphs and Oceanides retired
To grots and sacred groves, with loitering steps,
And bosoms swelled and throbbing, like a bird's
Held between human hands. The hounds with tongues
Crimson, and lolling hot upon the green,
And outstretched noses, flatly crouched; their skins
Clouded or spotted, like the field-bean's flower,
Or tiger-lily, painted the wide lawns.

Orion wandered deep into a vale
Alone; from all the rest his steps he bent,
Thoughtful, yet with no object in his mind;
Languid, yet restless. Near a hazel copse,
Whose ripe nuts hung in clusters twined with grapes,
He paused, down gazing, 'till upon his sense
A fragrance stole, as of ambrosia wafted

---

[47] Temple of Artemis
[48] Petrifying

Through the warm shades by some divinity
Amid the woods. With gradual step he moved
240 Onward, and soon the poppied entrance found
Of a secluded bower.[49] He entered straight,
Unconsciously attracted, and beheld
His Goddess love, who slept—her robe cast off,
Her sandals, bow and quiver, thrown aside,
245 Yet with her hair still braided, and her brow
Decked with her crescent light. Awed and alarmed
By loving reverence—which dreads offence
E'en though the wrong were never known, and feels
Its heart's religion for religion's self,
250 Besides its object's claim—swift he retired.

   The entrance gained, what thoughts, what visions his!
What danger had he 'scaped, what innocent crime,
Which Artemis might yet have felt so deep!
255 He blest the God of Sleep who thus had held
Her senses! Yet, what loveliness had glanced
Before his mind—scarce seen; Might it not be
Illusion?—some bright shadow of a hope
First dawning? Would not sleep's God still exert
260 Safe influence, if he once more stole back
And gazed an instant? 'Twere not well to do,
And would o'erstain with doubt the accident
Which first had led him there. He dare not risk
The chance 'Twere not illusion oh, if true!
265 While thus he murmured hesitating, slow,
As slow and hesitating he returned
Instinctively, and on the Goddess gazed!

   With adoration and delicious fear,
270 Lingering he stood; then pace by pace retired,
Till in the hazel copse sighing he paused,
And with most earnest face and vacant eye,
And brow perplexed, stared at a tree. His hands
Were clenched; his feet pressed down the soil,
275 And changed their place. Suddenly he turned round,
And made his way direct into the bower.

   There was a slumbrous silence in the air,
By noon-tide's sultry murmurs from without
280 Made more oblivious. Not a pipe was heard

---

[49] Shady, restful place

From field or wood; but the grave beetle's drone
Passed near the entrance: once the cuckoo[50] called
O'er distant meads, and once a horn began
Melodious plaint, then died away. A sound
285   Of murmurous music yet was in the breeze,
For silver gnats that harp on glassy strings,
And rise and fall in sparkling clouds, sustained
Their dizzy dances o'er the seething meads.
With brain as dizzy stood Orion now
290   I' the quivering bower. There rapturous he beheld,
As in a trance, not conscious of himself,
The perfect sculpture of that naked form,
Whose Parian[51] whiteness and clear outline gleamed
In its own hue, nor from the foliage took
295   One tint, nor from his ample frame one shade.
Her lovely hair hung drooping, half unbound,—
Fair silken braids, fawn-tinted delicately,
That on one shoulder lodged their opening coil.
Her large round arms of dazzling beauty lay
300   In matchless symmetry and inviolate grace,
Along the mossy floor. At length he dropped
Softly upon his knees, his clasped hands raised
Above his head, 'til by resistless impulse
His arms descending, were expanded wide
305   Swift as a flash, erect the Goddess rose!

    Her eyes shot through Orion, and he felt
Within his breast an icy dart. Confronted,
Mutely they stood, but all the bower was filled
310   With rising mist that chilled him to the bone,
Colder, as more obscure the space became;
And ere the last collected shape he saw
Of Artemis, dispersing fast amid
Dense vapoury clouds, the aching wintriness
315   Had risen to his teeth, and fixed his eyes,
Like glistening stones in the congealing air.

---

[50] Slender, often colorful birds, with strong legs
[51] Snow-white marble quarried from the Greek island of Paros

Zeus

"The Mythology of Greece and Rome: With Special Reference to Its Use,"
Otto Seemann, 1877, p. 27.

Book I

Canto the Third

O'ER plastic nature any change may come,
Save that which seeks to crush the primal germ;
And outward circumstance may breed within,
A second nature which o'ercomes the first,
But ne'er destroys, though dormant or subdued.
More toil for him whose wandering fancies teem
With too much life, and that vitality
Which eats into itself; more toil of brain
And limb, sole panacea for the change
From tyrant senses to pure intellect.
Wherefore, his work redoubled, Artemis
Directs Orion's course; not as before
With grave and all-subduing tenderness,
While with white fingers midst his chestnut locks,
In her speech pausing, gently would she hang
Violets, as white as her own hands, and sprigs
Of Cretan[52] dittany,[53] whose nodding spikes
Flushed deeper pink beneath the sacred touch,—
But with a penetrating influence
And front austere,[54] as suiting best the Queen
Of maiden immortality. His soul
Strove hard to ascend and leave the earth behind;
And by the Goddess' guidance every hour
Had its fixed duties. Husbandry of fields
She taught those giant hands, and how to raise
The sweetest herbs and roots, which now his food
Became; nor taste and culture of the vine
Permitted, nor of slaughtered kine the flesh,
Nor forest boar, nor other thing that owns
An animal life. Lastly, she taught his mind
To reason on itself, far as the bounds
Of sense external furnish images
And types in attestation of each phase
Of man's internal sphere—large orbit space
For varied lights—and also showed the way
Rightly his complex knowledge to employ,
And from their shadows trace substantial things,
Things back again to shadows—thus evolving
The principle of thought, from root to air.

---

[52] Crete: Largest Greek island
[53] Perennial, flowering plant of Crete that is called "love" on the island
[54] Bleak

         This done, the blossom and the fruit of all
      Was her prime truth, into each element
      Of his life's feelings and its acts, to instil:
      'Twas Love's divinest essence. In the soul,
45   Central its altar's flame for ever burns
      Inviolate, and knowing not the change
      Which time and fate o'er all else in the world
      Bring speedily, or with a creeping film
      That hides decay. Ever at peace it dwells
50   With its secure desires, which are soul-fed,
      Nor on idolatrous devotion made
      Dependent, nor on will and wayward moods
      Of others; 'Tis self-centred as a star,
      And in the music of the conscious nerves,
55   Finds bliss, which e'en the slightest touch or look
      Of this magnetic passion can create,
      And render perfect. Nor doth absence break
      The links of ecstasy, which from a heart
      By a heart are drawn, but midst the glare of day,
60   The depths of night, alone, or in a crowd,
      Imagination of love's balmy breath
      Can to the spirit fashion and expand
      Love's own pure rapture and delirium.
      To this fixed sublimation there belong
65   No conflicts of pale doubts, anxieties,
      Mean jealousies, anguish of heart-crushed slaves,
      And forlorn faces looking out on seas
      Of coming madness, from the stony gaps
      Through which departed truth and bliss have fled;
70   But high communion, and a rapturous sense
      Of passion's element, whereof all life
      Is made; and therefore life should ne'er attain
      A mastery o'er its pure creative light.

75   Midst chequered sunbeams through the glancing woods
      No more Orion hunted; from the dawn
      Till eve, within some lonely grot he sat,
      His thoughts reviewing, or beneath a rock
      Stood, back reclined, and watching the slow clouds,
80   As doth a shepherd in a vacant mood
      Oft to some highest peak would he ascend,
      And gaze below upon his giant friends,
      Who looked like moving spots, so dark and small;
      And oft, upon some green cliff ledge reclined,
85   Watch with sad eye the jocund chase afar

In the green landscape, where the quivering line
Led by the stag—who drew its rout behind
Of woodland shapes, confused as were their cries,
And sparkling bodies of fleet-chasing hounds,—
90 Passed like a magic picture, and was gone.
His husbandry soon ceased; he hated toil
Unvaried, ending always in itself,
And to the Goddess pleaded thoughtful hours
For his excuse, and indolent self-disgust.
95 Small profit found his thought; his sympathies
Were driven inward, and corroded there.

    Sometimes he wandered to the lowland fens,
Where the wild mares toss their sharp manes in the blast,
100 And scour through washy reeds and hollows damp—
Hardened in after ages by long droughts;
And midst the elements he sought relief
From inward tempests. Once for many hours,
In silence, only broken from afar
105 By the deep lowing of some straying herd,
Moveless and without speech he watched a hind[55]
Weeding a marsh; a brutish clod, half built,
Hog-faced and hog-backed with his daily toil,
Mudded and root-stained by the steaming ooze,
110 As he himself were some unnatural growth;
Who yet, at times, whistled through broken fangs—
"Happier than I, this hind," Orion thought.

    Once tow'rds the city outskirts strayed his steps,
115 With a half purpose some relief to seek
Midst haunts of men, and on the way he met
A mastic-sifter[56] with his fresh-oiled face.
"O friend!" Orion said, "why dost thou walk
With shining cheek so sadly in the sun?"
120 Sighing, the melancholy man replied:—
"The lentisk-trees[57] have ceased to shed their gums;
Their tears are changed for mine, since by that tree
Myself and children live. My toil stands still.
Hard lot for man, who something hath within

---

[55] Red, female deer
[56] Typically a duck or goose, but in this case a man who strains food from plants, in this instance an aromatic, evergreen shrub
[57] Mastic tree from which it pea-sized berries are cultivated for resin in chewing gum

125	More than a tree, and higher than its top,
	Or circling clouds, to live by a mere root
	And its dark graspings! Clearly I see this,
	And know how 'Tis that toil unequally
	Is shared on earth: but knowledge is not power
130	To a poor man alone 'gainst all the world,
	Who, meantime, needs to eat. Like the hot springs
	That boil themselves away, and serve for nought,
	Which yet must have some office, rightly used,
	Man hath a secret source, for some great end,
135	Which by delay seems wasted. Ignorance
	Chokes us, and time outwits us."—On he passed.
	"That soul hath greater cause for grief than I,"
	Orion thought—yet not the less was sad.
140	Away disconsolate the giant went,
	Now clambering forest slopes, now hurrying down
	Precipitous brakes, tearing the berried boughs
	For food, scarce tasted, and oft gathering husks,
	Or wind-eggs of strange birds dropt in the fens,[58]
145	To toss them in some rapid brook, and watch
	Their wavering flight. But now a tingling sound
	Wakes his dull ear!—a distant rising drone
	Upon the air, as of a wintry wind—
	And dry leaves rustle like a coming rain.
150	The wind is here; and, following soon, descends
	A tempest, which relieves its rage in tears.
	Kneeling he stooped, and drank the hissing flood,
	And wished the Ogygian deluge[59] were returned;
	Then sat in very wilfulness beside
155	The banks while they o'erflowed, till starting up,
	Bounding he sought his early giant friends.
	Them, in their pastoral yet half savage haunts
	Found, as of yore, he with brief speech addressed,
160	And bade them to an orgie on the plain,
	By rocks and forests amphitheatred.
	Such greeting high they with a gleeful roar
	Received, and forthwith rose to follow him,
	Save Akinetos, who seemed not to hear,
165	But looked more grave still seated on a stone,

---

[58] Wetlands
[59] Great flood of Greek mythology during the reign of Ogygian

While they betook them to the plains below.

    Thither at once they sped, and on the way
Rhexergon tore down boughs, while Harpax slew
170   Oxen and deer, more than was need; and soon
On the green space Orion built the pile
With cross logs, underwood, dry turf and ferns,
And cast upon it fat of kine, and heaps
Of crisp dry leaves; and fired the pile, and beat
175   A hollow shield, and called the Bacchic train,[60]
Who brought their skins of wine, and loaded poles
That bent with mighty clusters of black grapes
Slung midway. In the blaze Orion threw
Choice gums, and oil, that with explosion bright
180   Of broad and lucid flame alarmed the sky,
And fragrant spice, then set the Fauns to dance,
While whirled the timbrels, and the reed-pipes blew
A full-toned melody of mad delight.
Down came the Msenads[61] from the sun-brown'd hills,
185   And flocked the laughing Nymphs of groves and brooks;
With whom came Opis,[62] singing to a lyre,
And Sida,[63] ivory-limbed and crowned with flowers.
High swelled the orgie; and the roasting bulk
Of bull and deer was scarce distinguishable
190   'Mid the loud-crackling boughs that sprawled in flame.
Now richest odours rose, and filled the air—
Made glittering with the cymbals spun on high
Through jets of nectar upward cast in sport,
And raging with songs and laughter and wild cries!
195

    In the first pause for breath and deeper draughts,
A Faun who on a quiet green knoll sat—
Somewhat apart—sang a melodious ode,
Made rich by harmonies of hidden strings,
200   Unto bright Merope the island's pride,
And daughter of the king; whereto a quire
Gave chorus, and her beauties rare rehearsing,
Wished that Orion shared with her the throne.

---

[60] God of wine in Greek mythology
[61] Followers of Bacchus who took to revelry in the woods during special seasons
[62] Greek goddess of abundance
[63] Short for Cressida, meaning "The Golden One"

205   The wine ran wastefully, and o'er the ears
Of the tall jars that stood too near the fire,
Bubbled and leapt, and streamed in crimsoning foam,
Hot as the hissing sap of the green logs.
But none took heed of that, nor anything.
210 Thus song and feast, dance, and wild revelry,
Succeeded; now in turn, now all at once
Mingling tempestuously. In a blind whirl
Around the fire Biastor dragged a rout[64]
In osier bands[65] and garlands; Harpax fiercely
215 The violet scarfs and autumn-tinted robes
From Nymph and Msenad tore; and by the hoofs
Autarces seized a Satyr, with intent,
Despite his writhing freaks and furious face,
To dash him on a gong, but that amidst
220 The struggling mass Encolyon thrust a pine,
Heavy and black as Charon's ferrying pole,[66]
O'er which they, like a bursting billow, fell.

    At length when night came folding round the scene,—
225 And golden lights grew red and terrible,
Flashed torch and spear, while reed-pipes deeper blew
Sonorous dirgings and melodious storm,
And timbrels groaned and jangled to the tones
Of high-sustaining horns,—then round the blaze,
230 Their shadows brandishing afar and athwart
Over the level space and up the hills,
Six Giants held portentous dance, nor ceased
Till one by one in bare Bacchante arms,
Brim-full of nectar, helplessly they rolled
235 Deep down oblivion. Sleep absorbed their souls.

    Region of Dreams! ye seething procreant[67] beds
For germs of life's solidities and power;
Whether ye render up from other spheres
240 Our past or future beings to the ken[68]
Of this brief state; or, wiser, are designed,
With all your fleeting images confused,

---

[64] Throng or crowd of people
[65] Bands of willow branches
[66] Gondolier of Hades who ferries dead souls across River Styx using black pole
[67] Procreating
[68] Recognition

To scatter, during half our mortal hours,
The concentrating passions and the thoughts
245 Which else were madness; Oh maternal realm,
Console each troubled heart!—with opiate hand
Gently the senses charm, and lead astray
The vulture thoughts by thy blest phantasies,
Beckoning with vague yet irresistible smile!
250
    Sleep's God the prayer well pleased received, but said,
"Not such the meed of those who seek my courts
Through Bacchanalian orgies." O'er the brain
Of fallen Orion visions suitable
255 Came with voluptuous gorgeousness, preceded
By a dim ode; and as it nearer swelled,
In rapturous beauty Merope swept by,
Who on him gazed in ecstasy! He strove
To rise—to speak—in vain. Yet still she gazed,
260 And still he strove; till a voice cried in his ear,
"Depart from Artemis!—she loves thee not—
Thou art too full of earth!" He started awake!
The piercing voice that cast him forth, still rang
Within his soul; the vision of delight
265 Still ached along each nerve; and slowly turning
A look perplexed around the spectral air,
Himself he found alone 'neath the cold sky
Of day-break, midst black ashes and ruins drear.

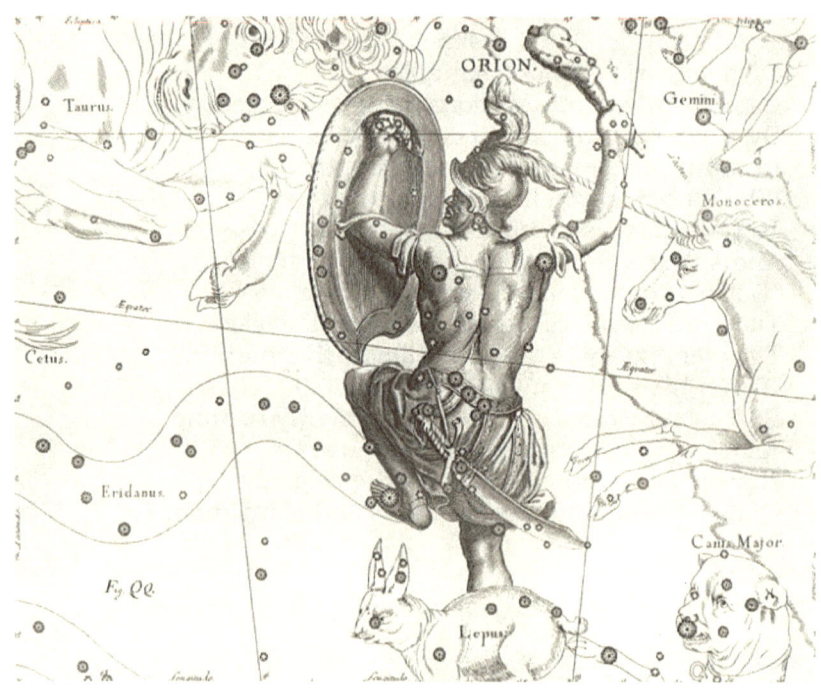

Orion

"Uranographia," Johannes Hevelius, 1690.

Orion

Book II

Book II

Canto the First

BENEATH a tree, whose heaped-up burthen swayed
In the high wind, and made a hustling sound,
As of a distant host that scale a hill,
Autarces and Encolyon gravely sat.
Sometimes they spake aloud, then murmured low,
Then paused as if perplexed,—looked round and snuffed
The odour of wood-fires in the fresh forest air,—
And then again addressed them to their theme.
Of cloudy-brained Orion they discoursed,
Lost to companionship, and led by dreams.

"Once," said Autarces, "he was great on earth;
A worker in iron, and a hunter fleet
Who oft ran down the stag; when, by some chance,
He pleaseth Artemis, and in her train,
All his high worth resigning, and his friends,
Dwindles to suit her fancy, and becomes
A giant of lost mind." Encolyon thrust
His heavy heel into the soil, and spake
With serious gesture. "Ever Orion sought
Some new device, some hateful onward deed
Through strange ways hurrying, scorning wise delay.
A victim fell he soon to Artemis
And her cold spells, for of his Ocean-sire
Orion's soul hath many a headlong tide.
But most of all her gleamy illusions fell
Upon his mind, which soon became a maze
For ghostly wanderings, and wild echoes heard
Through mists; and none could comprehend his speech."

"Methought the orgie had recalled his sense,
So fairly he bespake us to the mirth;
So full and giant-like was his disport
Throughout the night," Autarces now rejoined.
Encolyon raised one hand:— "That orgie's waste
Of energies," he murmured, "and the hours
Far better given to rest, I much deplore.
Why joined I in the mirth?—how was I lost!
But when a regulated mind sedate,
Its perfect poise permits to waver aside
One tittle, certainly the man must fall
Somewhat in dignity, howe'er retrieved.
Hence, when a regulated"— Here his speech
Autarces interrupted hastily,

45 Since, for his share, no self-reproach felt he.
    "I say the orgie, and his high disport,
    Shewed in Orion some return to sense:
    And when next morn I saw him near a brook,
    Where I had stooped to drink—by him unseen—
50 Down ran he like a panther close pursued,
    Then stopped and listened—now looked up on high-
    Now stared into the brook as he would drink,
    And drain its ripplings to the last white stone—
    Then went away forgetful. This methought,
55 E'en by its wildness and its strenuous throes,
    Savoured of hope, and of his safe return
    To corporal sense, by shaking off these nets
    Of moon-beams from his soul; but when I rose
    And crossed his path, and bade him speak to me,
60 Again 'Twas all of vapour and dark thoughts,
    Unlike the natural thoughts of bone and thews[69]
    As we of yore were taught, and found enough
    For all our needs, and for our songs and prayers,
    Yet had he, as it seemed, some plan within,
65 And ever tended to some central point
    In some place—nought more could I understand;
    Wherefore I deem that he is surely mad."
    "And so deem I," rejoined Encolyon;
    "Ever advancing—working a new way—
70 Tasking his heart, forgetful of his life
    And present good—of madness the sure sign."

       While thus they talked. Harpax with speed approached,
    shouting his tidings— "Merope loves Orion—
75 Orion hath gone mad for Merope!"
    The twain who had erewhile the cause discerned,
    And signs of reason's lost, at this fresh news,
    So little dreamed of from his recent mood,
    A minute looked each other in the face
80 With sheep-like gravity, then backward sank
    Against the tree, loud laughing. 'This were good,'
    Checking his laughter with a straight-lined face,
    Encolyon said, "if not too deeply burning.
    And that a power he hold within himself
85 To pause at will." But Harpax quick rejoined,
    "I, for myself, would have this Merope,
    And force Oinopion render up his crown,

---

[69] Strong muscle

If ye will aid me." "We will give our aid,"
Autarces cried__"and yet me thinks this love
90 Affecting doubly, as by the self-same blow,
Might from some spells in the orgie-fumes arise?
Ye marked, wise Akintos would not move."
"Doubtless 'Twas wise," Encollyon said. "More care
Befits our steps." They rose and strode away,
95

There is a voice that floats upon the breeze
From a heathed mountain; voice of sad lament
For love left desolate ere its fruits were known
Yet by the memory of its own truth sweetened,
100 If not consoled. To this Orion listens
Now, while he stands within the mountain's shade.

"The scarf of gold you sent to me, was bright
As any streak on cloud or sea, when morn
105 Or sunset light most lovely strives to be.
But that delicious hour can come no more,
When, on the wave-lulled shore, mutely we sat,
And felt love's power, which melted in fast dews
Our being and our fate, as doth a shower
110 Deep foot-marks left upon a sandy moor.
We thought not of our mountains and our streams
Our birth-place, and the home of our life's date,
But only of our dreams—and heaven's blest face.
Never renew thy vision, passionate lover—
115 Heart-rifled maiden—nor the hope pursue,
If once it vanish from thee; but believe
'Tis better thou shouldst rue this sweet loss ever
Than newly grieve, or risk another chill
On false love's icy river, which betraying
120 With mirrors bright to see, and voids beneath,
Its broken spell should find no faith in thee."

Thus sang a gentle Oread who had loved
A River-god with gold-reflecting streams,
125 But found him all too cold—while yet she stood
Scarce ankle-deep—and droopingly retired
To sing of fond hopes past. Orion's hand
A jeweled armlet held, where on his eyes
Earnestly rested. By a lovely boy,
130 Smiling, 'Twas brought to him while he reclined
Desponding, o'er a rock. "This gift, still warm,
My mistress sends thee, giant son of Ocean,

>   Once having seen thee in the hunting train
>   Of Artemis, Her name, if thou wouldst know,
> 135 Is Merope, daughter of Chio's king,
>   The proud Oinopion, lord of a hundred ships."
>
>   Orion to the palace of the king
>   Forthwith departed. Merope once seen,
> 140 His eyes resign their clear external power.
>   And see through feeling, utterly possessed
>   With her rare image; and his deep desire,
>   Deeper by energies so long confused,
>   When half his earth-born nature was subdued,
> 145 Struggled and bounded onward to the goal.
>
>   Her beauty awed the common race of men.
>   Her's was a shape made for a serpent dance,
>   Which charmed to stillness and to burning dreams,
> 150 But she herself the illusive charm o'erruled
>   As doth an element, merging for a time,
>   Ne'er lost; and none could steadily confront
>   Her sphinx-like bosom, and high watchful head.
>   Dark were her eyes, and beautiful as Death's
> 155 With a mysterious meaning, such as lurks
>   In that pale Ecstasy, the Queen of Shades
>   All deemed her passion was a mortal flame,
>   Volcanic, corporal, ending with its hour
>   Of sacrifice, dissolving in fine air;
> 160 Save one bald sage, who said that human nerves,
>   And what they wrought, were wondrous as the mind,
>   And in the eye of Zeus none could decide
>   Which held the higher place. For, to the nerves
>   Perfect abstraction and pure bliss belonged,
> 165 As parent of all life, and might in death
>   Continuance through some subtler medium find,—
>   Whence, life renewed, and heaven at length attained.
>
>   Nought of this sage's lore recked Merope,
> 170 And, for Orion, he was sick of thought,
>   Save that which round his present object played
>   Delicious gambols[70] and high phantasies.
>   Together they, the groves and templed glades
>   That, like old Twilight's vague and gleamy abode,
> 175 In mist and maze clung round the palace towers

---

[70] Frolicking

Roved, mute with passion's inward eloquence.
They loitered near the founts that sprang elate
Into the dazzled air, or pouring rolled
A crystal torrent into oval shapes
180 Of blood-veined marble; and oft gazed within
Profoundly tranquil and secluded pools,
Whose lovely depths of mirrored blackness clear—
Oblivion's lucid-surfaced mystery—
Their earnest faces and enraptured eyes
185 Visibly, and to each burning heart, revealed.
"And art thou mine to the last gushing drop
Of these high throbbing veins?" each visage said.
Orion straightway sought Oinopion's court,
And his life's service to the gloomy king
190 He proffered for the hand of Merope.

   Oinopion strode about his pillared hall,
And the dun chequers[71] of its marble floor
Counted perplexed, while pondering his reply.
195 Orion's strength and giant friends he feared;
Nor to accept the alliance, nor refuse,
Seemed wise. Thereto, Poseidon's empire rolled
Too near, and might surround his towers with waves;
Wherefore the king a double face assumed.
200 'Orion, I consent,' mildly he said:
Thy service I accept, and to thee give,
When thou shalt have performed it, Merope.
Clear me our Chios of its savage beasts,
Dragon and hippogrif,[72] wolves, serpents dire,
205 Within six days, and Merope is thine.'

   Through the high palace gates Orion passed,
Speeding to seek strong aid for this hard task
Among his forest friends. Old memories
210 Slumbrously hung above the purple line
Of distance, to the east, while odorously
Glistened the tear-drops of a new-fallen shower;
And sun-set forced its beams through strangling boughs,
Gilding green shadows, till it blazed athwart
215 The giant-caves, and touched with watery fires
The heavy foot-marks which had plashed[73] the sward[74]

---

[71] Brown to dull gray colors
[72] Head of an eagle, long talons, wings and torso of a horse
[73] Light splash

On vacant paths, through foliaged vistas steep,
Where gloom was mellowing to a grand repose.
At intervals, as from beneath the ground,
220 Far in the depth of these primeval cells,
Low respirations came. There, in great shade,
The giants sleep. Lost sons are they of Time.

There is no hour when rest is sacred held
225 By him who works and builds; and eve and night,
Alike with day, his toil oft-Times will claim.
"Awake companions! 'tis Orion calls!"
And straight the giants rose, and came to him,
Save Akinetos, into whose low cave
230 They with a torch now entered, there to hold
The conference, for he was very wise,
And ne'er proposed, nor did a thing that failed.

Orion's tale is told; Autarces then
235 For Merope proposed the lots to draw,
Whereat Orion glared,—but speech refrained
When Harpax fiercely on Autarces turned
With loud reproach, since he had sworn to him
Far different purpose; so Orion smiled,
240 And of Rhexergon and Biastor sought
Aid in his heavy task. They promised this—
When each one, by an arm, Encolyon
Grasped, and reminded of the darkness. "Night
Is the fit time," Orion cried, "to dig
245 The pitfalls, throw up mounds with bristling stakes
At top, as barriers, and the nets and toils
Fix and prepare, and choose our clubs and spears."
But still Encolyon urged a day's delay,
For dignity of movements thus combined,
250 If not for need. To Akinetos now
All turned with reverence, waiting the result
Of silent wisdom and of calm profound;
But from these small things he had long withdrawn
His godlike mind, and was again abstract.
255
Orion took the torch, and led the way
Into the dark damp air. Each to his post
Assigning; one, for the chief mountain pass,
Soon as the grey dawn touched the highest peaks;

---

[74] Meadow

260 One, in the plains below; two, for the woods;
The while Biastor and himself would range
The island, driving to the centre all
That should escape their spears.
'Twas thus resolved.
265 Meantime Rhexergon and Biastor joined
Orion, who went forth to dig the pits,
Break down high tops of trees, and weave their boughs
In barrier walls, and fix sharp stakes on mounds
And river banks. When they were gone, a yell,
270 Mocking the wild beasts doomed to be destroyed,
Harpax sent forth. "Mine be the task," he said,
"To ravage the King's pastures—slay his bulls—
And into our own woods and meadows drive
His goats and stags." "Rather collect alive,"
275 Autarces interposed, "with strong-meshed nets,
All the mad beasts, and loose them suddenly
Within (Oinopion's palace! That were sport
Worthy our toil; small joy for us to aid
Orion's freaks for love of Merope,—
280 Whom yet, methinks, he wisely hath preferred
To crystal-bosomed, wintry Artemis,—
Pale huntress, exiled from our sunny woods,
With crescent trembling bloody in eclipse,
Had my will power—" "But all her nymphs detained,
285 And, like our vines, of the ripe golden fruit
Deep rifled through their leaves," Harpax rejoined:
"Or placed," Encolyon muttered to himself,
"On pedestals, until they changed to stone,"—
And something worse he said, not safe to tell;—
290 "All votive statues to the Goddess famed
For cruel purity and marble heart—"
Autarces shouted, looking up on high.

    All this heard Artemis, who o'er the caves
295 Rolled her faint orb before the coming dawn,
In lonely sadness; and with an inward cry
Of jealous anguish and of vengeful ire,
Like an electric spark that knows not space,
Shot from her throne into the eastern heaven.

Hephaestus

"The Mythology of Greece and Rome: With Special Reference to Its Use,"
Otto Seemann, 1877, p. 27.

Book II

Canto the Second

THE Sun-god's tresses o'er the whirling reins
That scarcely ruled the swift-ascending steeds,
Fell, like a golden torrent, while his head,
Answering his goddess sister's brief request,
5   Smiling he bowed,—and the clouds closed behind
His blazing wheels. Four of those giant's sires
Were gods, who with their earth-born sons might hold
Communion; wherefore Artemis, alone,
Deemed not her power sufficed for safe revenge;
10 Of which now sure, her course to earth she bent.

The night-work done, his friends Orion left
Their further preparations to complete,
And to the caves returned, hopeful that now
15 The others would assist. There sat the three,
Listening the slow speech of Encolyon,
Who with change-hating eyes, fixed on the earth,
Discoursed, and to Orion's anxious looks
Thus made reply. "We have resolved to give
20 Our utmost aid—or aid that may suffice,—
In furtherance of thy task, which many days
Rightly requires." "Six days," Orion said,
And turned to go; when Harpax interposed:
Be it then six, but our conditions hear.
25 Take Merope, thy prize; the rest be ours.
(Oinopion's kingdom we shall duly share,
And make Encolyon king, as fitted best
For cares of state and governance of men."
"Not altogether King," Encolyon said
30 With meekness— "but, in sooth, I would return
Among mankind, and dictate to small towns."

Orion answered, "This were breach of faith
In me; the King and all his subjects, still
35 Must as I found them rest, until he die;
Then, as ye will, among ye take the crown,
Which, having Merope, I ne-er shall claim
Away now to our work." Autarces rose.
"This we accept," he said, "for brief is life
40 Of man—and insecure. But further thought
Should prompt us rather choose Encolyon
As guiding minister and staid high priest,
While Akinetos rule as Chios's king."

45 At mention of the name so reverenced,
Silently all assented. "See, the light
Of day spreads warmly down the valley slopes!"
Orion cried. Now Phoibos through the cave
Sent a broad ray! Harpax arose, and then,—
50 Pondering on rules for safest monarchy,—
Encolyon heavily. The solar beam
Filled the great cave with radiance equable,[75]
And not a cranny held one speck of shade.
A moony halo round Orion came,
55 As of some pure protecting influence,
While with intense light glared the walls and roof,
The heat increasing. The three giants stood
With glazing eyes, fixed. Terribly the light
Beat on the dazzled stone, and the cave hummed
60 With reddening heat, till the red hair and beard
Of Harpax shewed no difference from the rest,
Which once were iron-black. The sullen walls
Then smouldered down to steady oven-heat,
Like that with care attained when bread has ceased
65 Its steaming, and displays an angry tan.
The appalled faces of the giants shewed
Full consciousness of their immediate doom.
And soon the cave a potter's furnace glowed,
Or kiln for largest bricks, and thus remained
70 The while Orion, in his halo clasped
By some invisible power, beheld the clay,
Of these his early friends, change. Life was gone!

  Now sank the heat—the cave-walls lost their glare—
75 The red lights faded, and the halo pale
Around him, into chilly air expanded.
There stood the three great images, in hue
Of chalky white and red, like those strange shapes
In Egypt's ancient tombs; but presently
80 Each visage and each form with cracks and flaws
Was seamed, and the lost countenance brake up,
As, with brief toppling, forward prone they fell,—
And in dismay uttering a sudden cry,
Orion headlong from the cavern fled.
85

---

[75] Unvarying

     Fierce Harpax, and wind-steered Autarces, smitten
     From life thus early, may by few be wept;
     But long laments by the chief rulers made.
     Of Chios, for the sage Encolyon,
90   Far echoed, and still echo through the world—
     Which feels, e'en now, for his great principle
     A secret reverence. "Chainer of the wheel!
     Hater of all new things!—to whom the acts
     Of men seemed erring ever in each hope
95   And effort to advance, save in a round,
     Taught by the high example of the spheres!—
     Oh champion grave, who with a boundary stone
     Stood'st in improvement's door-way like a god,
     Ready by wholesome chastisement to grant
100 Crushing protection; regulator old
     Of science, scorning genius and its dreams,
     And all the first ideas and germs of things,
     Time and his broods of children shall prolong
     Thy fame, thy maxims, and thy practise staid,
105 Fraught with experience turning on itself."

     O'er the far rocks, midst gorge and glen profound;
     Now from close thickets, now from grassy plains;
     The sounds of raging contest, flight and death,
110 Told where Rhexergon and Biastor wrought
     Their well-directed work. Them, quickly joined
     Their head in this destruction, and ere night,
     Huge forms, ferocious, mighty in the dawn,
     When hoar rime[76] glistened on each hairy shape,
115 Nought fearing, swift, brimfull of raging life,
     Lay stiffening in black pools of gellied gore.
     Nor with the day ceased their tremendous task,
     But all night long Orion led the way
     Through moonless passes to most secret lairs,
120 Where in their deep abodes fierce monsters crouched,—
     Dragons, and sea-beasts, and compounded forms,—
     And in the pitchy blackness madly huddling,
     Midst deafening yell and hisses they were slain.

125   Next day the unabated toil displayed
     Like prowess and result; but with the eve
     Fatigue o'ercame the giants, and they slept.
     Dense were the rolling clouds, starless the glooms,

---

[76] Frost

But o'er a narrow rift, once drawn apart,
130 Shewing a field remote of violet hue,
The high Moon floated, and her downward gleam
Shone on the upturned giant faces. Rigid
Each upper feature, loose the nether jaw;
Their arms cast wide with open palms; their chests
135 Having like some large engine. Near them lay
Their bloody clubs with dust and hair begrimed,
Their spears and girdles, and the long-noosed thongs.
Artemis vanished; all again was dark.

140 　　With day's first streak Orion rose, and loudly
His prone companions called. But still they slept.
Again he shouted; yet no limb they stirred,
Though scarcely seven strides distant. He approached,
And found the spot, so sweet with clover flower
145 When they had cast them down, was now arrayed
With many-headed poppies, like a crowd
Of dusky Ethiops[77] in a magic cirque,
Which had sprung up beneath them in the night,
And all entranced the air. Orion paced
150 Around their listless bodies thoughtfully.
"Three giants slain outright by Phoibos's beams,—
Now hath a dead sleep fallen on my friends.
'Twas wise in Akinetos not to move."
An earthquake would not wake them. Artemis
155 Rejoices, and the hopes of Merope,
To whom the news a breathless shepherd bore,
Throbbed fearfully suspended o'er the brink
Of this event. Not long Orion paused:
"Though all may fail, the utmost shall be tried:
160 Secure is he who on himself relies."
This, hastening to his work, was all he said.

　　Four days remain. Fresh trees he felled, and wove
More barriers and fences; inaccessible
165 To fiercest charge of droves, and to o'erleap
Impossible. These walls he so arranged,
That to a common centre each should force
The flight of those pursued; and from that centre
Diverged three outlets. One, the wide erpanse,
170 Which from the rocks and inland forests led;
One, was the clear-skied windy gap above

---

[77] Black iron

    A precipice; the third, a long ravine
    Which, through steep slopes, down to the sea shore ran
    Winding, and then direct into the sea.

175
    Two days remain. Orion, in each hand
    Waving a torch, his course at night began,
    Through wildest haunts and lairs of savage beasts.
    With long-drawn howl, before him trooped the wolves,—
180 The panthers, terror-stricken,—and the bears
    With wonder and gruff rage; from desolate crags
    Leering hyaenas, griffin,[78] hippogrif,
    Skulked, or sprang madly, as the tossing brands
    Flashed through the midnight nooks and hollows cold,
185 Sudden as fire from flint; o'er crashing thickets,
    With crouched head and curled fangs, dashed the wild boar,
    Gnashing forth on with reckless impulses,
    While the clear-purposed fox crept closely down
    Into the underwood, to let the storm,
190 Whate'er its cause, pass over. Through dark fens,
    Marshes, green rushy swamps, and margins reedy,
    Orion held his way,—and rolling shapes
    Of serpent and of dragon moved before him
    With high-reared crests, swan-like yet terrible,
195 And often looking back with gem-like eyes.
    All night Orion urged his rapid course
    In the vexed rear of the swift-droving din,
    And when the dawn had peered, the monsters all
    Were hemmed in barriers. These he now o'erheaped
200 With fuel through the day, and when again
    Night darkened, and the sea a gulf-like voice
    Sent forth, the barriers at all points he fired,
    Midst prayers to Hephaestus and his Ocean-sire.

205   Soon as the flames had eaten out a gap
    In the great barrier fronting the ravine
    That ran down to the sea, Orion grasped
    Two blazing boughs; one high in air he raised,
    The other with its roaring foliage trailed
210 Behind him as he sped. Onward the droves
    Of frantic creatures with one impulse rolled
    Before this night-devouring thing of flames,
    With multitudinous voice and downward sweep
    Into the sea, which now first knew a tide,

---

[78] Head and wings of an eagle, long talons, torso of a lion

215	And, ere they made one effort to regain
	The shore, had caught them in its flowing arms,
	And bore them past all hope. The living mass
	Dark heaving o'er the waves resistlessly,
	At length, in distance, seemed a circle small,
220	Midst which, one creature in the centre rose,
	Conspicuous in the long red quivering gleams
	That from the dying brands streamed o'er the waves.
	It was the oldest dragon of the fens,
	Whose forky flag-wings and horn-crested head
225	O'er crags and marshes regal sway had held;
	And now he rose up, like an embodied curse
	From all the doomed, fast sinking—some just sunk—
	Looked land-ward o'er the sea, and flapped his vans,[79]
	Until Poseidon drew them swirling down.
230	
	Along the courts and lofty terraces,
	Within Oinopion's palace echoing,
	The choral voices and triumphal clang
	Of music, ordered by the royal maid,
235	Advanced to greet Orion. She with flushed neck
	And arms; large eyes of flashing jet and fire,
	And raven tresses fallen from their bands,
	The loud procession led. But soon they met
	A phalanx[80] armed with mandate from the king,
240	And all the triumph ceased. Oinopion
	Gnawed on his lip, and gathered up his robe
	In one large knot. Forthwith the whispering guards
	His daughter to the strongest tower convey;
	Then silently return. Orion comes:
245	"The work is done, O king! and Merope
	My bride, I claim—my second father thou!"
	This said, he bent his knee. With wandering eye,—
	Like one who seems to seek within the air
	An object, while his thoughts would gather time
250	For guile—and with averted face, the king
	Answered, "Thou claim'st too soon!"—and inwardly
	Oinopion said— "Three of his giant band
	Are dead; the others spell-bound sleep." The voice
	Of wronged Orion rose within the hall,
255	Demanding Merope; but image-like,
	Hard as if hewn out from a flinty cliff,

---

[79] Wings
[80] Long formation of infantry with long spears and swords

And stately stood the king, as he replied,
"She waits the voice of our mute oracles."

260   In a deep forest where the night-black spires
Of pines begin to swing, and breathe a dirge
Whose pauses are filled up with yearning tones
Of oaks that few external throes display
Midst their robust unyielding boughs—the winds
265 Are flying now in gusts, and soon a storm
Bursts howling through them, like a Fury sent
In quest of one who hath outstripped his fate
And been caught up to heaven. But no escape
Or premature release his course attends
270 Whose passions boil above mortality;
Nor till those mortal struggles have transpired
Can satisfaction or repose be found.
Vainly shall he with self-deluding pride
Of weakness, masked with power, seek solitude
275 And high remoteness from his fellow men,
In all their bitter littleness and strife;
Their noble efforts, suffering martyrdom.
He conquers not who flies, except he bear
Conquest within; nor flies he who believes
280 The object of his passion he can grasp,
Save for design to consummate the end.

"Oh, raging forest, do I seek once more
Your solitude for my secure abode?"
285 Orion cried, with wild arms cast abroad,
Fronting a tree whose branches lashed the air,
While its leaves showered around;—"And shall I not
In your direct communion with the earth
And heavens, find sympathy with this branched frame
290 I bear, thus shaken; yet unlike your storm
Which may be wholesome, coming from without,
And from the operative round of things,
While mine is centred in myself, and rends
But does not remedy. Let me then shun
295 The baleful[81] haunts of men—worse than the beasts
Whom I have exiled, and to shadows changed—
Savage as beasts with less of open force;
As wily, with less skill and promptitude;
As little reasoning, save for selfish ends;

---

[81] Harmful or ominous

300 Less faithful, true, and honest, than the dog;
     But hypocritical, which beasts are not,
     Save in the fables which men make for them!
     Into myself will I henceforth retire,
     And find the world I dreamed of when a child.
305 Nor this alone; but worlds of higher mould
     And loftier attributes shall roll before
     My constant contemplation, in the cave
     Of Akinetos, whom at times I'll seek,
     And emulate his wisdom; ever right
310 In never moving, more than absolute need.
     Thus shall I find my solace in disdain
     Of earth's inhabitants, whom through city and field
     I've found sheer clay, save in the visions bright,
     Of Goddess, and of Nymph,—0 Merope!
315 And where art thou, while idly thus I rave?
     Runs there no hope—no fever through thy veins,
     Like that which leaps and courses round my heart?
     Shall I resign thee, passion-perfect maid,
     Who in mortality's most finished work
320 Rank'st highest—and lov'st me, even as I love?
     Rather possess thee with a ten-fold stress
     Of love ungovernable, being denied?
     'Gainst fraud what should I cast down in reply?—
     What but a sword, since force must do me right,
325 And strength was given unto me with my birth,
     In mine own hand, and by ascendancy
     Over my giant brethren. Two remain,
     Whom prayers to dark Hephaestus and my sire
     Of ocean, shall awaken into life;
330 And we will tear up gates, and scatter towers,
     Until I bear off Merope. Sing on!
     Sing on, great tempest! in the darkness sing!
     Thy madness is a music that brings calm
     Into my central soul; and from its waves
335 That now with joy begin to heave and gush,
     The burning Image of all life's desire,
     Like an absorbing fire-breathed phantom-god,
     Rises and floats!—here touching on the foam,
     There hovering over it; ascending swift
340 Star-ward, then swooping down the hemisphere
     Upon the lengthening javelins of the blast!
     Why paused I in the palace groves to dream
     Of bliss, with all its substance in my reach?
     Why not at once, with thee enfolded, whirl

345   Deep down the abyss of ecstasy, to melt
        All brain and being where no reason is,
        Or else the source of reason? But the roaring
        Of Time's great wings which ne'er had driven me,
        By dread events nor broken-down old age,
350   Back on myself, the close experience
        Of false mankind, with whispers cold and dry
        As snake-songs midst stone hollows, thus has taught me—
        The giant hunter, laughed at by the world,—
        Not to forget the substance in the dream
355   Which breeds it. Both must merge in one.
        Now shall I overcome thee, body and soul,
        And like a new-made element brood o'er thee
        With all devouring murmurs! Come, thou storm,
        And clasp the rigid pine—this mortal frame
360   Wrap with thy whirlwinds, rend and wrestle down,
        And let my being solve its destiny,
        Defying, seeking, thine extremest power,
        Famished and thirsty for the absorbing doom
        Of that immortal death which leads to life,
365   And gives a glimpse of heaven's parental scheme."

Book II

Canto the Third

IN parching summer, when the mulberry leaves
Drooped broad and gleaming, and the myrtles curled,
While the pomegranate's rind grew thin and hard;
The vegetation of the isle looked pale,
Flaccid, and fading in despondency
For rain, and the young corn in every field,
With dry and rustling murmur as it waved,
Glistened impatiently, till autumn's tomb
Received the husky voice, and spring's dead hopes.
The vine-hills, and wild turpentines that grew
Along the road beneath, all basked content,
As did the lentisk-trees; but many a pant
And sultry sigh came from the fields and meads,
The city's gardens, where no fountains played,
And hot stone temples in the sacred groves.
Such lack of moisture oft had been endured,
And e'en the latest winter, whose thick breath
Solemnly wafted o'er the Ægean sea,
Had not resigned a single peak of snow
To melt and flow down for the brooks of spring.

   But since the breath of spring had stirred the woods,
Through which the joyous tidings busily ran,
And oval buds of delicate pink and green
Broke, infant-like, through bark of sapling boughs,—
The vapours from the ocean had ascended,
Fume after fume, wreath upon wreath, and floor
On floor, till a grey curtain upward spread
From sea to sky, and both as one appeared.
Now came the snorting and precipitous steeds
Of the Sun's chariot tow'rds the summer signs;
At first obscurely, then with dazzling beams;
And cleared the heavens, but held the vapours there,
In cloudy architecture of all hues.
The stately fabrics and the eastern pomps,
Tents, tombs, processions veiled, and temples vast,
Remained not long in their august repose,
But sank to ruins, and re-formed in likeness
Of monstrous beasts in lands and seas unknown.
These gradually dilating, limb from limb,
And head from bulk, were drawn apart, and floated
Hither and thither, till in ridges strewn,
Like to a rich and newly-furrowed field,
Then breaking into purple isles and spots,

45 Faded to faintness, and dissolved in air.

One midnight dark a spirit electric came,
And shot an invisible arrow through the sky,
Which instantly the wide-spread moisture called
50 To congregate in heavy drops, that fell
As suddenly. Like armies, host on host,
Pouring upon the mountains, vales, and plains,
The showers clashed down. Each runnel and thin stream
A branching brook became, or flowing river;
55 Each one small river rolled a goodly flood
With laughing falls, and many a Naiad[82] bright
And rush-crowned Hirer-god, was newly born,
While all the land-veins with fresh spirit ran
In this quick season of Orion's life.
60
The snows on every height had drank the showers,
Till heavy with the moisture, each steep ridge
Lost its pure whiteness and transparent frost;
Sank down as humbly as a maid once proud,
65 Who droops and kneels and weeps; and from beneath
Its stagnant foam melted quick running rills
Down slopes, with sunny music and loud hum,
Precipitous, ere through dark craggy rifts
Sparkling it dashed, and poured towards the plain.
70 Unusual growth of corn was in the land,
Whose fields with tender-flowing greenness smiled,
As winds with shades ran dances over them;
And e'en the vineyards, oliveyards, and groves
Of citron, were in their abundant fruits
75 Abundantly increased: all works increased.

Dark as an eagle on a cloudy rock,
(Oinopion sat upon his ancient throne.
Fixed was his face, while, through a distant gate,
80 Upon the ruins of a tower he gazed,
That like a Titan's[83] shattered skeleton
Still in its place stuck fast. But she was gone
His daughter Merope was borne away;
And willingly he knew; and whither fled,
85 He knew. But how recover, or revenge
The loss?—new dangers, outrage, how avert?

---

[82] Nymph in Greek mythology that rules over streams and rivulets
[83] God of ancient Greece until dethroned by Zeus

Infuriate were his people at the deed,
For by the giants many had been slain,
Ere they had won their prize. 'Gainst Merope,
90   Some spake aloud; against Orion, all,—
Save the bald sage, who said "'Twas natural."
"Natural!" they cried, "O wretch!" The sage was stoned.

    Within his cave, in his accustomed place,
With passive dignity that ever holds
95   Unwise activity in check and awe—
And active wisdom where the will's not strong—
Sat Akinetos, listening to the tale
Thus by Rhexergon told; Biastor leaning
Against a rock, with folded arms, the while.

100   "We from our trance with aching brows awoke
Starting, and on our elbows raised, with chins
Set in our hands, collected our mazed minds.
We both had dreamed one dream. In Chios's walls
A feast we held in honour of the king,
105   Encolyon, newly chosen—as we thought—
By the chief rulers, while Orion stood
Chained to the throne. But Merope, 'twas said,
Should still be his, if loyal, hand and soul.
Yet ere Orion answered, rushing came
110   A small dark shape—some airy messenger—
Darting on all sides, diving, nestling, leaping,
Swift as a mullet[84] coursing the sea hare,
And strong, as when within the shore-hauled net
It searches, like a keen hound, to and fro,
115   And no gap finding, bounds o'er the high-drawn line,
One leaps—all follow like a flock of sheep
Over a wattle.[85] So, this headlong sprite,[86]
Which, in our dream, now multiplied to shoals,[87]
And thus confused the feasters. But what 'twas
120   None saw, nor knew; but all the feast they marred,
While, in the place of meats and fruits, we found
Dust—dry-baked dust; the dust of the gone king,
Encolyon—as a bird in the air screamed forth—

---

[84] Stout and quick fish
[85] Fence intertwined with figs and branches
[86] Elfish being
[87] Large grouping

By Phoibos smitten. Now a sound we heard,
Like to some well-known voice in prayer; and next
An iron clang that seemed to break great bonds
Beneath the earth, shook us to conscious life.
A briny current passing through our hearts
Stung all our faculties back to former power;
And as we rose, across a distant field
We saw Orion coming with a sword.
Our dream thus ended in reality
Without a boundary line. What followed seemed
Continuous, for Orion urged us on.
Fresh work had he in hand; few words explained;
And to (Oinopion's city we repaired,
Entering at eve of a great festival,
I with a club, iron bound, of ponderous weight;
Biastor with a shield, forged by Orion,
Whose disk enormous would protect all three,
And, set with ray-like spikes around the rim,
Looked like a fallen star. Onward we drove
Behind this threatening orb, down-trampling all
Who fled not, or our impulse strove to oppose;
Feasters and dancers, chieftains, priests, and guards;
I tell it as it happened—blow by blow—
Till near a high tower, doubtful of our course
At bay, like bulls, within a circle clear
By terror made, we paused. The archers soon,
With bow-arm forward thrust, on all sides twanged,
Around, below, above. Behind the shield
That on its spikes stood grimly, we retired,
And heard the rattling storm; when from the tower
A light flashed down one side, and at the top
Stood Merope, who cried, 'Orion, see!
My prison I have fired, and in my haste
Fired first below. I cannot pass the flames!'
E'en while she spake a hydra-wreath[88] of smoke
Ran coiling up the stony stair, and peered
Into each chamber with its widening head,
As if to seek its prey. Again she cried—
'I will leap down into thine arms!' 'Forbear!'
Shouted Orion. 'First let us try our strength
With skill.' I on the groaning gate-posts smote,
Until their bolts and nails started like tusks
From battered jaws, and inward sunk the gates,

---

[88] Lernaean hydra is a snakelike water creature with multiple heads

Crushing armed men behind. O'er all we passed.
Orion, now in front, amidst a cloud
Of smoke, dust, slaughter and confusing cries,
170   The blackened slabs of winding stair ascended;
And, in the same fierce uproar and dismay
Of men, not fit to cope with sons of Gods,
Unscathed came down with Merope. 'Twas good.
He bore her to the cedar grove afar,
175   Where in brief space a palace he had built,
While we, remaining midway, called a rout
Around us, and great revel held that night."

    Rhexergon ceased, while in the sunny air
His large eyes shone, and, pleased with what he told—
180   For well he spake with deep-voiced cadences—
Looked like a monarch who hath made a verse.
Now Akinetos spake. "Your efforts done,
What good to ye is wrought? To him, what good?
Not long will Merope be his: if long,
185   What good, since both must tire. (Oinopion,
The king of ships and armies, may reclaim
This Merope by force: perchance her own
Inconstant will may save these ships and men."
"If we defend the prize," Biastor said
190   "Substantial good unto ourselves were due;
Wise are thy words; wherefore large terms of spoil
We with Orion will in future make,
That shall secure our constant revelry,
As in Dodona,[89] once, ere driven thence
195   By Zeus, for that Rhexergon burnt some oaks.
Thrust we the king from off his throne, or thrust
His throne from under him to some fresh place
Suiting our fancies, whereon we'll sleep crowned,
And feast, and order armies to march forth,
200   And ships to sail, and music, and more feast."

    "Better pull down the city, and destroy
The fleet"—Rhexergon said— "Then, all despoiled—
And made as slaves,—leave we our woodland homes:
There live, with Akinetos for our king?
205   Aught we destroy Orion can rebuild,

---

[89] Northwestern Greece where oracle of Mother Goddess (earth) presided

If we should need; or frame aught else we need;
Rise, therefore, Akinetos, thou art king!"
So saying in his hand he placed a spear.

    As though against a wall 'twere set aslant,
210 Flatly the long spear fell upon the ground.
"He will not be a king; nor will he aid
Your purposes," murmured the Great Unmoved.
"Autarces, Harpax, aided, and both died;
Orion's work will shortly work his end;
215 Encolyon, ever meddling to prevent,
Wasted his mind and care, and found his death.
Those who have wisdom aid not, nor prevent.
Nought good has followed aught that ye have done,
Nor will good follow aught that ye can do,
220 Or I can do, or any one can do,
Except such good as of itself may come,
If so 'twas ordered. Leave God to his work,
The Supreme Mover of all things, and best,
Who, if we move not, must himself sustain
225 His scheme: hence, never moved by hands unskilled,
But moved as best may be. Be warned; sit still."

    Within the isle, far from the walks of men,
Where jocund chase was never heard, nor hoof
Of Satyr[90] broke the moss, nor any bird
230 Sang, save at times the nightingale—but only
In his prolonged and swelling tones, nor e'er
With wild joy and hoarse laughing melody,
Closing the ecstasy, as is his wont,—
A forest separate and far withdrawn
235 From all the rest, there grew. Old as the earth,
Of cedar was it, lofty in its glooms
When the sun hung o'er head, and, in its darkness,
Like Night when giving birth to time's first pulse.
Silence had ever dwelt there; but of late,
240 Came faint sounds with a cadence regular
From the far depths, as of a cataract
Whose echoes midst incumbent foliage died.
From one high mountain gushed a flowing stream,
Which through the forest passed, and found a fall
245 Within, none knew where, then rolled tow'rds the sea.

---

[90] Woodland friends of Pan and Dionysus

There underneath the boughs, mark where the gleam,
Of sun-rise through the roofing's chasm is thrown
Upon a grassy plot below, whereon
The shadow of a stag stoops to the stream
250   Swift rolling towards the cataract, and drinks deeply.
Throughout the day unceasingly it drinks,
While ever and anon the nightingale,
Not waiting for the evening, swells his hymn—
His one sustained and heaven-aspiring tone—
255   And when the sun hath vanished utterly,
Arm over arm the cedars spread their shade,
With arching wrist and long extended hands,
And grave-ward fingers lengthening in the moon,
Above that shadowy stag whose antlers still
260   Hung o'er the stream. Then came a rich-toned voice
Out of the forest depths, and sang this lay,
With deep speech intervalled and tender pause.

"If we have lost the world what gain is ours!
Hast thou not built a palace of more grace
265   Than marble towers? These trunks are pillars rare,
Whose roof embowers with far more grandeur. Say;
Hast thou not found a bliss with Merope,
As full of rapture as existence new?
'Tis thus with me. I know that thou art blest.
270   Our inmost powers—fresh winged shall soar and dream
In realms of Elysian[91] gleam, whose air—light—flowers,
Will ever be—though vague, most fair—most sweet—
Better than memory.—Look yonder, love!
What solemn image through the trunks is straying?
275   And now he doth not move, yet never turns
On us his visage of 'rapt vacancy!
It is Oblivion.[92] In his hand—though nought
Knows he of this—a dusky purple flower[93]
Droops over its tall stem. Again, ah see!
280   He wanders into mist, and now is lost.__
Within his brain what lovely realms of death

---

[91] Elysian fields are the beautiful fields that serve as the final resting place of the just and heroic
[92] Typically called Lethe, one of the rivers of Hades that represents forgetfullness
[93] Asphodel, or flower of death, Asphodel Meadows serve as a resting place for ordinary people in Hades

       Are pictured, and what knowledge through the doors
       Of his forgetfulness of all the earth,
       A path may gain? Then turn thee, love, to me:
285   Was I not worth thy winning and thy toil,
       O, earth-born son of Ocean! Melt to rain."

         No foot may enter 'midst these cedar glooms:
       Passion is there—a spell is on the place—
290   It hath its own protecting atmosphere,
       Needing no walls nor bars. But Chios's king
       Hath framed his purpose; the sworn instruments
       Chosen; and from the palace now depart
       In brazen chariots, richly armed, ten chiefs.
295   "Watch well your moment!"—lastly spake the king;
       "Slay not outright—but make his future life
       A blot—a blank!" They bent their plumed helms,
       And through the gates in thunder whirled away.

         Beyond the cedar forest lay the cliffs
300   That overhung the beach, but midway swept
       Fair swelling lands, some green with brightest grass,
       Some golden in the sun. Mute was the scene,
       And moveless. Not a breeze came o'er the edge
       Of the high-heaving fields and fallow lands;
305   Only the zephyrs at long intervals
       Drew a deep sigh, as of some blissful thought,
       Then swooned to silence. Not a bird was seen
       Nor heard: all marbly gleamed the steadfast sky.
       Hither Orion slowly walked alone,
310   And passing round between two swelling slopes
       Of green and golden light, beheld afar
       The broad grey horizontal wall o' the dead-calm sea.

         O'ersteeped in bliss; prone on its ebbing tide;
       With hope's completeness vaguely sorrowful,
315   And sense of life-bounds too enlarged; his thoughts
       Sank faintly through each other, fused and lost,
       Till his o'ersatisfied existence drooped;
       Like fruit-boughs heavily laden above a stream,
       In which they gaze so closely on themselves,
320   That, touching, they grow drowsy, and submerge,
       Losing all vision. Sense of thankful prayers
       Came over him, while downward to the shore
       Slowly his steps he bent, seeking to hold

Communion with his sire. The eternal Sea
325 Before him passively at full length lay,
As in a dream of the marmoreal[94] heavens.
With hands stretched forward thus his prayer began;
"Receive Poseidon!—but no further words
Found utterance. And again he prayed, and said,
330 "Receive, O Sire;"—yet still the emotion rose
Too full for words, and with no meaning clear.
He turned, and sulking on a sandy mound,
With dim look o'er the sea, deeply he slept.

335   What altars burn afar—what smoke arises
Beyond the swelling lands above the cliffs?
Or is it but a rolling cloud of dust
That onward moves, driven by the wind? And now
A rumbling sound is gathering in the breeze,
340 And nearer swells—now dies away—like wheels
That pass from stony ground to grassy plains.
Again!—it rings and jars—and passing swift
Along the cliffs, till lost in a ravine,
Five brazen chariots fling the sunset rays
345 Angrily back upon the startled air!
In one, the last, struggles a lovely form,
Half pinioned[95] by a chieftain's broidered scarf,
Her wild black tresses coiling round an arm
Which still she raises, striving to make a sign.
350 All disappeared. No voice, no sound was heard.
The moon arose—and still Orion slept,—
The profound sleep of life's satiety,[96]
In him whose senses else had quick regained
The sure protection of his healthy powers.
355
    Forth from a dark chasm issue figures armed.
Close conference they hold, like ravens met
For ominous talk of death. No more: their shields,
Plumed helms, and swords, two chieftains lay aside,
360 Then stoop, and softly creep tow'rds him who sleeps;
While o'er their heads the long protecting spears
Are held by seven, who noiselessly and slowly

---

[94] Resembling marble or having its qualities of material or color whiteness
[95] Restrained
[96] Satisfaction

        Follow their stealthy progress. Step by step
        The deadly crescent moves behind the twain,
365   Who, flat as reptiles, and with face thrust out,
        Breathless, all senses sharpen. Now!—'Tis done!
        The poison falls upon the dreamer's lids.

           Away, aghast at their own evil deed,
        As though some dark curse on themselves had fallen,
370   Flashed the mailed moon-lit miscreants into shade,
        Like fish at sudden dropping of a stone.
        The Moon now hid her face. The sea-shore lay
        In hollowness beneath the rising stars,
        And blind Orion, starting at once erect
375   Amid his darkness, with extended arms
        And open mouth that uttered not a word,
        Stood statue-like, and heard the Ocean moan.

Pan

"The Mythology of Greece and Rome: With Special Reference to Its Use,"
Otto Seemann, 1877, p. 130.

Orion

Book III

Book III

Canto the First

THERE is an age of action in the world;
An age of thought; lastly, an age of both,
When thought guides action and men know themselves,
What they would have, and how to compass it.
5   Yet are not these great periods so distinct
Each from the other,—or from all the rest
Of intermediate degrees and powers,
Cut off,—but that strong links of nature run
Throughout, and prove one central heart, wherein
10 Time beats twin-pulses with Humanity.
In every age an emblem and a type,
Premature, single, ending with itself,
Of future greatness in an after-time,
May germinate, develop, radiate,
15 And like a star go out and leave no mark
Save a high memory. One such is our theme.

    The wisdom of mankind creeps slowly on,
Subject to every doubt that can retard,
20 Or fling it back upon an earlier time;
So timid are man's footsteps in the dark,
But blindest those who have no inward light.
One mind, perchance, in every age contains
The sum of all before, and much to come;
25 Much that's far distant still; but that full mind,
Companioned oft by others of like scope,
Belief, and tendency, and anxious will,
A circle small transpierces and illumes:
Expanding, soon its subtle radiance
30 Falls blunted from the mass of flesh and bone.
The man who for his race might supersede
The work of ages, dies worn out—not used,
And in his track disciples onward strive,
Some hairs'-breadths only from his starting point:
35 Yet lives he not in vain; for if his soul
Hath entered others, though imperfectly,
The circle widens as the world spins round,—
soul works on while he sleeps 'neath the grass.
So, let the firm Philosopher renew
40 His wasted lamp—the lamp wastes not in vain,
Though he no mirrors for its rays may see,
Nor trace them through the darkness;—let the Hand
Which feels primeval impulses, direct
A forthright plough, and make his furrow broad,

45   With heart untiring while one field remains;
       So, let the herald Poet shed his thoughts,
       Like seeds that seem but lost upon the wind.
       Work in the night, thou sage, while Mammon's brain[97]
       Teems with low visions on his couch of down;—
50   Break, thou, the clods while high-throned Vanity,
       Midst glaring lights and trumpets, holds its court;—
       Sing, thou, thy song amidst the stoning crowd,
       Then stand apart, obscure to man, with GOD.
       The poet of the future knows his place,
55   Though in the present shady be his seat,
       And all his laurels deepening but the shade.

       But what is yonder vague colossal shape,
       That like a burthened giant bending moves,
60   With outspread arms groping its upward way
       Along a misty hill? In the blear shades,
       Sad twilight, and thick dews darkening the paths
       Whereon the slow dawn hath not yet advanced
       A chilly foot, nor tinged the colourless air—
65   The labouring figure fades as it ascends.

       'Twas he, the giant builder-up of things,
       And of himself, now blind; the worker great,
       Who sees no more the substance near his hands,
70   Nor in them, nor the objects that his mind
       Desires and would embody. All is dark.
       It is Orion now bereft of sight,
       Whose eyes aspired to luminous designs.
       The sun and moon and stars are blotted out,
75   With their familiar glories, which become
       Henceforth like chronicles remote. The earth
       Forbids him to cleave deep and trace her roots,
       And veins, and quarries: Whose wide purposes
       Are narrowed now into the safest path:
80   Whose lofty visions are all packed in his brain,
       As though the heavens no further could unfold
       Their wonders, but turned inward on themselves;
       Like a bright flower that closes in the night
       For the last time, and dreams of by-gone suns
85   Ne'er to be clasped again: Thou art reduced
       To ask for sympathy and to need help;

---

[97] A brain filled with the desire for wealth

       Stooping to pluck up pity from all soils-
       Bitterest of roots that round pride's temple grow—
       Losing self-centred power, and in its place
90   Pressed with humiliation almost down:
       Whose soul had in one passion been absorbed,
       Which, though illimitable in itself,
       Profound and primal, yet had wrapped him round
       Beyond advance, or further use of hand,
95   Purpose and service to the needy earth:
       Whose passion, being less than his true scope,
       Had lowered his life and quelled aspiring dreams,
       But that it led to blindness and distress,
       Self-pride's abasement, more extensive truth,
100   A higher consciousness and efforts new.

       In that dark hour when anguished he awoke,
       Orion from the sea-shore made his way,
       Feeling from cliff to cliff, from tree to tree,
105   Guided by knowledge of the varied tracks
       Of land,—the rocks, the mounds of fern, the grass,
       That 'neath his feet made known each spot he passed,—
       Hill, vale and woodland; till he reached the caves,
       Once his rude happy dwelling. All was silent.
110   Rhexergon and Biastor were abroad,
       Searching the jasper[98] quarries for lynx
       That had escaped the wreck. Deeply he sighed.
       The quiet freshness came upon his heart,
       Not sweetly but with aching sense of loss.
115   He felt his way, and listened at the cave
       Of Akinetos, whom he heard within
       Sing to himself. And Akinetos rose,
       Perceiving he was blind, and with slow care
       Rolled forth a stone, and placed him by his side.
120
       Orion's tale soon closed; its outward acts
       And sad results, were all that he could speak:
       The rest writhed inwardly, and,—like the leads
       That sink the nets and all the struggles hide,
125   Till a strong hand drags forth the prize,—his words
       Kept down the torment, uttered all within
       In hurrying anguish. Yet the clear, cold eye,
       Grey, quiet, steady, of the Great Unmoved,

---

[98] Reddish gemstone

Saw much of this beneath, and thus he spake.

    "My son, why wouldst thou ever work and build,
And so bestir thyself, when certain grief,
Mischief, or error, and not seldom death,
Follows on all that individual will
Can of itself attain. I told thee this:
Nor for reproach repeat it, but to soothe
Thy mind with consciousness that not in thee
Was failure born. Its law preceded thine:
It governs every act, which needs must fail—
I mean, give place—to make room for the next.
Each thinks he fails, because he thinks himself
A chain and centre, not a link that runs
In large and complex circles, all unknown.
Sit still. Remain with me. No difference
Will in the world be found: 'twill know no change,
Be sure. Say that an act hath been ordained?
Some hand must do it: therefore do not move:
An instrument of action must be found,
And you escape both toil and consequence,
Which run their rounds with restless fools; forever
One act leads to another, and disturbs
Man's rest, and Reason—which foresees no end."

    "I feel that thou art wise" Orion said;
  "The worker ever comes to thee cast down!
Who with alacrity[99] would frame, toil, build,
If he had wisdom in results, like thee?
Would Strength life's soil upheave, though close it clung,
And heavy, like a spade that digs in clay,
Therein to plant roots certain not to grow?
Oh miserable man! Oh fool of hope!
All I have done has wrought me no fixt good,
But grief more bitter as the bliss was sweet,
Because so fleeting. Why did Artemis
Me from my rough and useful life withdraw?
O'er wood and iron I had mastery,
And hunted shadows knowing they were shades.
Since then, my intellect she filled, and taught me
To hunt for lasting truth in the pale moon.
Such proved my love for her; and such hath proved
My love for Merope, to me now lost.

---

[99] Eagerness

I will remain here: I will build no more."

He paused; but Akinetos was asleep.
175 Wherefore Orion at his feet sank down,
Tired of himself, of grief, and all the world,
And also slept. Ere dawn he had a dream:
'Twas hopeful, lovely, though of no clear sense
He said, "Methinks it most betoken good;
180 Some help from Artemis, who may relent,
And think of me as one she sought to lift
To her own sphere of purity; or, indeed,
Some God may deem me worthy of a fate
Better than that which locks up all design
185 In pausing night. Perchance, the dream may bode
That Merope shall be to me restored,
And I see nature through her death-deep eyes,
And know the glorious mysteries of the grave,
Which through extremes of blissful passion's life
190 Methought I saw. Oh wherefore am I blind?"
"Abandon all such hopes of Merope,"
Murmured the Great Unmoved: "her truth was strong,
First to herself, and through herself to thee,
While that it lasted; but that's done and gone.
195 How should she love a giant who is blind,
And sees no beauty but the secret heart
Panting in darkness? That is not her world."
Orion rose erect. "She is not false—
Although she may forget. I will go forth:
200 I may find aid, or cause some help to come
That shall restore my sight." The sage replied,
"Thou'st seen enough already, and too much
For happiness. This passion prematurely
Endeth; and therefore endeth as seems best,
205 Ere it wear out itself with languor and pain,
Or prostrate all thy mind to its small use—
Far worse, methinks." "Hast thou," Orion cried,
"No impulses—desires—no promptings kind?"
The sage his memory tasked; then slow replied:
210 "Once I gave water to a thirsty plant:
'Twas a weak moment with us both. Next morn
It craved the like—but I, for 'Nature' calling,
Passed on. It drooped—then died, and rotted soon,
And living things, more highly organized
215 With quick eyes and fine horns, reproached my hand
Which had delayed their birth. What wrong we do

By interfering with life's balanced plan!
Do nothing—wait—and all that must come, comes!"
Silent awhile they stood. Orion sighed,
"I know thy words are wise—" and went his way.

    The blindness of their leader, and his woe,
Now had Rhexergon and Biastor learnt,
And thoughts of plunder cried out for revenge,
Which on Oinopion they proposed to wreak,
And make good pastime round his ruined throne.
"Revenge is useless" Akinetos said:
"It undoes nothing and prevents repentance
Which might advantage others." Both replied,
"Thou speakest truth and wisdom;" and at eve
Departed for the city, bent to choose
Some rebel cheiftains for their aid, or slaves,
Or robbers who inhabited the rocks
North of the isle. A great revenge they vowed.

    And where was Merope? The cruel deed
Her sire had compassed for Orion's fall,
Smote through her full breast, and at every beat
Entered her heart; nor settled there, but coursed
Through all her veins in anguish. Her despair
Was boundless, many days, until her strength
Worn with much misery and the need of sleep,
Gave way, and slumber opened 'neath her soul,
Like an abyss. The deed, beyond recall,
Was done. She woke, and thought on this with grief.
The cruel separation, and the loss
Of sight, had been completed. Nothing now
Of passion past remained but memory,
Which soon grew painful; and her thoughts oft turned
For some relief, to listen to the songs
That minstrels sung, sent by the youthful king
Of Syros,[100] rich in pastures and in corn.
Beardless he was, dwarf-shaped, and delicate,
Freckled and moled, with saffron tressses fair;
Yet were his minstrels touched with secret fires,
And beauty was the theme of all their lays.
Of her they sung—sole object of desire—
And with rare presents the pale king preferred
His suit for Merope. Her sire approved;—

---

[100] Most agriculturally abundant Greek island

260 Invited him;—he came;—and Merope
With him departed in a high-beaked ship;
And as it sped along, she closely pressed
The rich globes of her bosom on the side,
O'er which she bent with those black eyes, and gazed
265 Into the sea that fled beneath her face.

All this Orion heard: his blind eyes wept.
Now was each step a new experiment;
Within him all was care; without, all chance;
270 Dark doubts sat in his brain; danger prowled round.
He wandered lost and lone, and often prayed,
Standing beside the tree 'neath which he slept,
And would have offered pious sacrifice,
But that himself a victim blindly strayed.
275 His forehead's dark with wrinkles premature
Of vexing action; his cheek scored all down
With debts of will that never can be paid;
Chagrin, pain, disappointment, and wronged heart.
At length, one day, some shepherd as he passed,
280 With voice that mingled with the bleat of lambs,
Cried, "Seek the source of light!—begin anew!"

On went he thinking, pausing, listening,
Till sounds smote on his ear, whereby he knew
285 That near the subterranean palace gates
Which for Hephaestus he of iron had framed,
His feet approached. He entered there, and found
Brontes, the cyclops, whom he straight besought
His shoulders to ascend, and guide his course
290 Eastward, to meet the Morning as she rose.
'Twas done. Their hazy forms erewhile we saw.

Swift down the misty eastern hill, whose top
Through broken vapours, swooning as they creep
295 Along the edges into the wide heavens,
Shews Morn's first ruddy gleam, a shape uncouth,
And lumbering forward in half-falls and bounds,
Comes with tossed arms! The Cyclops hoar with rime,[101]
His coarse hair flying, through the wet woods ran,
300 And in the front of Akinetos's cave
Shouting with gladness and resounding life,
Performed a hideous but full-hearted dance.

---

[101] Covered in frost

"Dance, rocks and forests! Akinetos dance!
The Worker and the Builder hath his sight!
Ho! ho! come forth—with either eye he sees!
Come forth, O Akinetos—laugh ye rocks!"

A shadow o'er the face of him who sat
Within that cave, passed,—lightly wrinkling
The ledge-like brow, which, though of granite, smoothed,
Not vexed, by ocean's tempests, now relaxed,
As it would say, "I pity this return
Of means for seeking fresh distress;"—and then
The broad great features their fixed calm resumed.

'Twas thus Orion fared; and this the scene.
Fast through the clouds retiring, the pale orb
Of Artemis a moment seemed to hang
Suspended in a halo, phantom-like,
Over a restless sea of jasper fire,
While bending forward tow'rds the eastern mount,
She gazed and hearkened. Soon the fervent voice
Of one who prayed beneath amid the mist,
Rose thrilling on the air; and onward slow
Her car its voyage held, and waned more pale
And distant, as the prayer ascended heaven.

"Eos![102] blest Goddess of the Morning, hear
The blind Orion praying on thy hill,
And in thine odorous breath his spirit steep,
That he, the soft gold of thy gleaming hand
Passing across his heavy lids, sealed down
With weight of many nights, and night-like days,
May feel as keenly as a new-born child,
And, through it, learn as purely to behold
The face of nature. Oh restore my sight!"

His prayer paused tremulous. O'er his brow he felt
A balmy beam, that with its warmth conveyed
Divine suffusion and deep sense of peace
Throughout his being; and amidst a pile,
Far in the distance, gleaming like the bloom
Of almond trees seen through long floating halls
Of pale ethereal blue and virgin gold,
A Goddess, smiling like a new-blown flower,

---

[102] Winged Greek goddess of the dawn

          Orion saw! And as he gazed he wept.
          The tears ran mingling with the morning dews
          Down his thick locks. At length once more he spake.

350   "Blest Eos! mother of the hopeful star,
          Which I, with sweet joy, take into my soul;
          Star-rays that first played o'er my blinded orbs,
          E'en as they glance above the lids of Sleep,
          Who else had never known surprise, nor hope,
355   Nor useful action; Golden Visitant,[103]
          So lovely and benign, whose eyes drove home
          Night's foulest ghosts, and men as foul; who bring'st
          Not only my redemption, but who art
          The intermediate beauty that unites.
360   The fierce Sun with the Earth, and moderates
          His beams with dews and tenderness and smiles;
          O bird-awakener giver of fresh life,
          New hopes, or to old hopes new wings,—receive
          Within thy care, one who with many things
365   Is weary, and though nought in energy
          Abated for good work, would seek thine aid
          To some fresh course and service for his hand;
          Of peace, meantime, and steadfast truth, secure!"

---

[103] Specter

Poseidon

"The Mythology of Greece and Rome: With Special Reference to Its Use,"
Otto Seemann, 1877, p. 103.

Book III

Canto the Second

L<small>EVEL</small> with the summit of that eastern mount,
By slow approach, and like a promontory[104]
Which seems to glide and meet a coming ship,
The pale gold platform of the morning came
5 Towards the gliding mount. Against a sky
Of delicate purple, snow-bright courts and halls,
Touched with light silvery green, gleaming across,
Fronted by pillars vast, cloud-capitalled,
With shafts of changeful pearl, all reared upon
10 An isle of clear aerial gold, came floating;
And in the centre, clad in fleecy white,
With lucid lilies in her golden hair,
Eos, sweet Goddess of the Morning, stood.

15 From the bright peak of that surrounded mount,
One step sufficed to gain the golden floor,
Whereon the Palace of the Morning shone,
Scarcely a bow-shot distant; but that step,
Orion's humbled and still mortal feet
20 Dared not adventure. In the Goddess's face
Imploringly he gazed. "Advance!" she said,
In tones more sweet than when some heavenly bird,
Hid in a rosy cloud, its morning hymn
Warbles unseen, wet with delicious dews,
25 And to earth's flowers, all looking up in prayer,
Tells of the coming bliss. "Believe—advance—
Or, as the spheres move onward with their song
That calls me to awaken other lands,
That moment will escape which ne'er returns."
30 Forward Orion stepped: the platform bright
Shook like the reflex of a star in water
Moved by the breeze, throughout its whole expanse;
And e'en the palace glistened fitfully,
As with electric shiver it sent forth
35 Odours of flowers divine and all fresh life.
Still stood he where he stepped, nor to return
Attempted. To essay one pace beyond,
He felt no power— yet onward he advanced
Safe to the Goddess, who, with hand outstretched,
40 Into the palace led him. Grace and strength,
With sense of happy change to finer earth,

---

[104] Tract of land that overlooks the ocean

Freshness of nature, and belief in good,
Came flowing o'er his soul, and he was blest.
'Tis always morning somewhere in the world,
45 And Eos rises, circling constantly
The varied regions of mankind. No pause
Of renovation and of freshening rays
She knows, but evermore her love breathes forth
On field and forest, as on human hope,
50 Health, beauty, power, thought, action and advance.
All this Orion witnessed, and rejoiced.
The turmoil he had known, the late distress
By loss of passion's object, and of sight,
Were now exchanged for these serene delights
55 Of contemplation, as the influence
That Eos wrought around for ever, dawned
Upon his vision and his inmost heart,
In sweetness and success. All sympathy
With all fair things that in her circle lay,
60 She gave, and all received; nor knew of strife;
For from the Sun her cheek its bloom withdrew,
And, ere intolerant noon, the floating realm
Of Eos—queen of the awakening earth—
Was brightening other lands, wherefrom black Night
65 Her faded chariot down the sky had driven
Behind the sea. Thus from the earth upraised,
And over its tumultuous breast sustained
In peace and tranquil glory—oh blest state!—
Clear-browed Orion, full of thankfulness,
70 And pure devotion to the Goddess, dwelt
Within the glowing Palace of the Morn.

But these serene airs did not therefore bring
A death-sleep o'er the waves of memory,
75 Where all its clouds and colours, specks of sails,
Its car-borne Gods, shipwrecks and drowning men,
Passed full in view; yet with a mellowing sense
Ideal, and from pain sublimed. Thus came
Mirrors of nature to him, and full oft
80 Downward on Chios turned his happy eyes,
With grateful thoughts that o'er life's sorrows wove
The present texture of a sweet content,
Passing all wisdom, or its rarest flower.
He saw the woods, and blessed them for the sake
85 Of Artemis; the city, and rich gloom

          That o'er the cedar forest ever hung,
          He also blessed for Merope; the isle,
          And all that dwelt there, he with smiles beheld,—
          Nor, it may be, without prophetic thrill
90   When on Mount Epos[105] turned his parting glance.
          There, in an after age, close at its foot,
          In the stone level was a basin broad
          Scooped out, and central on a low shaft sat
          A sage with silver hair, and taught his school,
95   Where the boy Homer[106] on the stony rim
          Sat with the rest around. Bright were his eyes.

          With re-awakened love, and sight enlarged
          For all things beautiful, and nobly true.
100   To the great elements that rule the world,
          Orion's mind, left to itself, reviewed
          Past knowledge, and of wisdom saw the fruit
          Far nearer than before, the path less rough,
          The true possession not austere and cold,
105   But natural in its strength and balance just
          Of body and of soul; each to respect,
          And to the other minister, and both
          Their one harmonious being to employ
          For general happiness, and for their own.
110   Such was the lore which now his thoughts attained,
          And he to Eos ventured to display,
          Beseeching her response? She only gazed
          With an approving smile upon the earth,
          That rolled beneath, and rendered back the gleam
115   With tender radiance over many a field.
          The story of his life Orion told—
          His youth—his labours—lastly of his loves;
          Nor what for Artemis his opening soul
          Had felt—what deep desire for Merope—
120   Sought to conceal. How much his intellect,
          And entire nature, owed to the pale Queen
          Of night's illumined vault, with grateful sighs
          Of reverential memory he declared;
          To Eos turning with a pleading look,
125   Lest she might not approve. She took his hand,
          And placed it on her side beneath her heart,
          Which beat a sphery music audibly.

---

[105] Mountain on the Greek island of Scio
[106] Ancient Greek poet, wrote "Illiad" and "Odysey"

He, listening, still enraptured, countless echoes,
Rang sweetly faint from distant groves beneath
130 Upon the earth. Within his hurrying heart
The trembling echoes now Orion felt,
And silent stood as one who apprehends
Some new and blissful hope that round him soars,
Which still eludes his vision and his mind.

135   Not in like doubt was Artemis, whose car—
Blank as it passed away before the morn,
Herself invisible—collapsed and yearned
Beneath the Goddess' spurning foot. At once
The lasting love of Eos she foresaw,
140 When at the tale of other loves he told
Sincerely, fully, with kind memories rife,
Orion's hand she pressed. His earnest eyes
All filled with new born light, she also read,
As in a mirror where the future's writ—
145 And, reading, closed her own as she retired.

   Meantime Rhexergon through the Chian streets[107]
Triumphant, with Biastor and a host
Of rebel chieftains and their armed bands,
And drunken slaves and robbers, drove the king
150 From his lost throne. Beyond the suburb fields
Oinopion fled, and secret refuge found
Among the tombs, beneath a chain of hills,
Where dense cold gloom his robe and crown became,
While over-head along the hillsides ran
155 The sunny vines. Tumult now choaked the city
With adverse crowds, and deafened it with cries
Of slayers, and of those who fled or fell.
The giants led the slaughter, oft commencing
Pillage, then turning yet again to slay,
160 Having no plan. They paused but to blaspheme
The Gods, like giants doomed to die. Rich spoil
Was found, seized, left—and trampled into mire
By feet that onward sprang for other spoil,
Or to tear down, wrench, overthrow, destroy;
165 Till thus Rhexergon rendered up his life.
All the chief rulers, priests, and sages old,
And heroes most renowned, Rhexergon vowed

---

[107] Streets of Chios

	Within the temple of Zeus to congregate;
	Wall up each means of egress, and from a gap
170	Made in the roof, pour down a rocky hail
	From broken fanes, cliff, quarry and sea-beach,
	Upon their heads; nor cease the rattling shower
	Until the temple was filled up with stones.
	To make the gap, he with his club advanced,
175	Where central, 'neath the roof, a pillar rose,
	Which was its main support, Blow upon blow
	He smote; the base gave way; the pillar fell;
	And with it fell the roof, and buried him.
	With equal skill Biastor wrought his fate.
180	On a long terrace, which precipitously
	Looked down on suburb gardens deep below,
	Near to the edge upon a pediment stood
	A great gilt statue to Encolyon,
	By the high rulers reverently set up;
185	And this inscription bearing on its base;—
	"To the Wheel-chainer! Reiner-in of steeds!
	August[108] preserver of revered decay;
	Votive[109]—erected by a people's love."
	Biastor, covered with a brazen shield,
190	Whirling his sword, and seeing not his way,
	A panic-stricken crowd before him drove
	On tow'rds the parapet.[110] Thence to escape,
	Some desperately rush back—are cloven down—
	The rest throng round the statue. It was carved
195	Of wood, and at its flat square base the sun
	Had often turned a scornful glance, and made
	Dry flaws, wherein had crept and nestled, rot.
	They cling around its knees!—the giant Force
	Comes like a mighty wind;—and, as a mast
200	In shipwreck, black with rigging flanking loose,
	And black with wild-haired creatures clinging round,
	With crash and horrid slant its blasted tree
	Surrenders sidelong,—so the statue fell.
	With it the crowd were carried; after it
205	Biastor, knowing not the depths beyond,

---

[108] Majestic
[109] Love offering
[110] Railing

        Or his strong impulse having no power to check,
Followed head foremost. Down the hollow banks
He, floundering o'er the statue's 'tangled coil,
Into an orchard 'midst the vale below,
210   Deep in the mould lay prone;[111] and over him
The fallen statue lay athwart. 'Twas thus,
The Builder absent, and at that time blind,
Force, and the Breaker-down their course fulfilled.

215   "What have I done on earth?" Orion said,
While pensive on the platform of the morn
He stood. " My youth's companions are destroyed,
And Akinetos evermore seems right,
Predicting failure to our human acts:
220   Or good, or ill, alike untoward prove.
I have not well directed mine own strength,
Nor theirs." As thus he mused, a skylark sang
Within the gleaming Palace, and a voice
Followed melodious as it spake these words.

225   "Well hast thou striven, and due reward shalt find;
For though reward held dalliance[112] with thy hopes
Of former days, and for thyself thou wrought'st,
The suffering and the lesson have sufficed
To fit thee for more noble aims. Sigh not
230   That those companions of thine unformed youth,
Their rude career have closed: evil was all
They could have done without thee. Thou hast won
The love of Eos; doubt not of her truth,
And to thyself be constant, as to her."

235   He turned, and at his side the Goddess smiled,
With tenderness of grace, such as the soul
Can through the heart convey, where both accord
One object to exalt. Orion knelt,
And looked up in her face, then rose and clasped
240   Her yielding loveliness. As they retired,
An eye glanced fire-like through the clear blue air,
And saw the embrace!—and marked the glowing beams
On Eos' bosom, rosy yet all gold,
Like ripened peaches in the morning light.

---

[111] Facedown
[112] Flirtation

245 That eye grew deadly—flashed—and it was gone,
As onward in its course the Palace moved.
'Twas Artemis!—beware her fatal dart.

O'er meadows green or solitary lawn,
When birds appear earth's sole inhabitants,
250 The long clear shadows of the morning differ
From those of eve, which are more soft and vague,
Suggestive of past days and mellowed grief.
The lights of morning, even as her shades
Are architectural, and pre-eminent
255 In quiet freshness, midst the pause that holds
Prelusive energies. All life awakes.
Morn comes at first with white uncertain light
Then takes a faint red, like an opening bud
Seen through grey mist: the mist clears off; the sky
260 Unfolds; grows ruddy; takes a crimson flush;
Puts forth bright sprigs of gold,—which soon expanding
In saffron, thence pure golden shines the morn;
Uplifts its clear bright fabric of white clouds,
All tinted, like a shell of polished pearl,
265 With varied glancings, violet gleam and blush;
Embraces Nature; and then passes on,
the Sun to perfect his great work.

So came thy love upon Orion's heart,
Oh life-awakening Queen of early light,
270 And the devotion he, at first, had deemed
All spiritual, now quickened, glowed, attained
Entire vitality, and that highest state
Which every noblest faculty employs
With self-enjoyment and beneficence.

275 True happiness no idle course endures,
But by activity renews its strength,
Which else would fail, and happiness revolve
Within itself, still dwindling to the point
Where pain first stings. Far otherwise it fared
280 With thee, Orion. Watchful tow'rds the world
His eye oft turned. The pure realm where he dwelt
Absorbed not all his sympathies in itself,
Which yet sprang forth, and sighed o'er ills below;
Like one uplifted in abstraction's mood,
285 Who sits alone, and gazes in the fire,

        Watching red ruins as they fall and change
        To glorious fabrics,—which forthwith dissolve,
        Or by some hideous conflict sink to nought,
        While from a black mass issues tawny smoke,
290   Followed by a trumpet flame. War, and the waste,

        So far as individual life and purpose feels,
        Of human labour,—both its hand and heart—
        Came crowding on his mind. Nor less his eye
        Earth's loveliness perceived; nor less his thoughts
295   Of Eos, who in all his fresh designs,
        Feelings, and wishes, shared, and urged him on
        With constant impulse, hidden in sweet smiles,
        And perfect love that thinks not of itself;—
        Conscious, contented, sphered beyond fresh hopes.
300   Earth was their child; and constant morn their home.

          Three things Orion contemplated oft:
        The first, his gratitude to Artemis
        Inspired; its general service and import
        To human happiness, a duty made.
305   Her temple in Delos darkened to the east
        With towering trees, amidst whose hollowed roots
        Dwelt poisonous Harpies.[113] These to dislodge, destroy;
        And hew the trees down, that the morning light,
        Followed by radiant warmth, might penetrate
310   Its depths, even to the temple's central shine,
        He purposed. Thus would Eos give her love
        To Artemis, and all be reconciled.

          His second purpose this: beneath the earth,
        So might the Father of the Gods give aid,
315   To build a dungeon for the God of War,
        Wherein, confined in a tumultous sleep,
        The visions of his madness should present
        The roar of battles and its sanguine joys,
        Its devastations, glories, and vain graves.
320   Here might he gloat on death, while o'er his head
        The sea-wide corn fields smiled in golden waves.

          The last, would need Poseidon's trident hand,
        Which, fervent prayers and filial offerings

---

[113] Monster with head and torso of a woman, wings and talons of bird

                Would fail not to obtain; whereby a blow,—
325   Such as had lifted out of the frothed sea
                Delos,—Kalliste,[114] with its fathomless bay,—
                Mountains, and coral rocks,—repeated oft,
                Might many mountains cause at once to rise,
                Higher and higher, till their summits kissed
330   The clouds. Then Eos, casting forth her robe
                From peak to peak, and her immortal breath
                Combining and sustaining that bright floor,
                A web of perfect skill, and guileless art,
                Unlike the dark artificers below,—
335   Large space for mortals of the earth would thus
                Be lifted to the platform of the morn.
                There, by the Goddess beckoned, and beholding
                Her face, divine in youth, the lengthened toil
                Of the ascent were but a test of worth,
340   And hollow sounds of roaring from the sea
                Beneath, cause none, who should ascend, to fall.

                    To Delos now Orion made descent
                With Eos, hand in hand, when lofty Night
                Advanced her shadowy shoulder on the sky.
345   Good speed made he with his well-practised hand;
                The Harpies slew; the eastward trees hewed down;
                And laid the temple open to the morn,
                With all her genial beams. Then Eos first
                Felt doubt; and trembled as she saw the fane
350   Gleam with her presence, glancing like the light
                Within an angry eye-ball. A keen breeze
                Now whistled all around, and as it rose
                The high green corn, like rapids tow'rds a fall,
                Flowed, wave on wave, before the strenuous wind.
355   She gazed with a cold cheek, till underneath
                The sea, she heard the coming Sim rejoice;
                And felt the isle for blest events prepare.
                Yet was she silent. The untended Sun,
                While Eos lingered midst the southern groves,
360   Made Delos vocal to its lowest roots.
                Yet stood she with Orion in the shade,
                Who noting not her tender, anxious face,
                In generous feelings happy, took his rest.

---

[114]Greek island

      Midst songs and garlands and uplifted joy,
365 Day's bright dream sped. Night came; but not the Moon.
      Night passed. Two spectral armies in the air
      Appeared, and with mute fury fought; then died
      In mist. A cloud of pale and livid blue,
      Lit from behind, hangs low amid the west!

370   What scarce-apparent ray! what wavering light
      Down glances, arching through the silent vault!
      Again it flies!—and yet again the ray!
      The omen and the deed unite—in death!
      Slain is Orion! slain is the Friend of Man!
375 Into the grove, and to the self-same spot
      The darts flew! They thy naked breast have reached,
      O, Giant! child-like in thy truthfulness,
      Yet full of noblest gifts, and hard-earned skill:
      Cut off when love was perfect, and in the midst
380 Of all thy fresh designs for human weal,
      To make the morning feel itself in vain,
      And men turn pale who never shed a tear!
      Thy task is finished—thou can'st work no more—
      Thy Maker takes thee, for he loved thee well.

385   Haggard and chill as a lost ghost, the Morn,
      With hair unbraided and unsandalled feet,—
      Her colourless robe like a poor wandering smoke,—
      Moved feebly up the heavens, and in her arms
      A shadowy burden heavily bore; soon fading
390 In a dark rain, through which the sun arose
      Scarce visible, and in his orb confused.

Book III

Canto the Third

STRONG Spirit of Nature! if with pious hand,
Of all humanity sensitive, and true
To the first heart of childhood, thou hast striven
Good to effect, and seemingly hast failed,
5   Lament it not; that impulse on the frame
Of the dense earth, which no result displays,
Effect or consciousness, not utterly
Shall turn aside, and glancing into space
Be lost and cast away. As with a thought
10   That, dormant in the brain well nigh a score
Of years, will suddenly, we know not how,
Rise bright before the mind, thus recognized
As that so long forgotten,—while two brains
Entire, have their material parts used up,
15   Given off, and changed for new;—so shall the deeds
Of virtuous power, in their appointed day,
Else with due strength above the buried hand
That called them first to light. Know this, and hope:
The earth has hard rind, but a subtle heart.
20   Therefore amidst those shadows, by no form
Projected; which in secret regions flit,
Of future being, through unnumbered states,
Which are most truly the substantial dreams,
Nor less the aspirations most unearthly,
25   Of man; shadows oft hunted, never caught,
Yet traced beyond the grave; to thought well known;
Amidst these shadows stride not thou forlorn,
O Giant sublime, whom death shall not destroy.

    'Twas eve, and Time his vigorous course pursuing,
30   Met Akinetos walking by the sea.
At sight of him the Father of the Hours
Paused on the sand,—which shrank, grew moist, and trembled
At that Unwonted pressure of the God.
And thus with look and accent stern, he spake.

35   "Thou art the mortal who, with hand unmoved,
Eatest the fruit of others' toil; whose heart
Is but a vital engine that conveys
Blood, to no purpose, up and down thy frame;
Whose forehead is a large stone sepulchre[115]

---

[115] Tomb

40　　Of knowledge! and whose life but turns to waste
　　　My measured hours, and earth's material!"

　　　　Whereto the Great Unmoved no answer made,
　　　And Time continued, sterner than before.
　　　"Thy sire, Tithonos,[116] living nine score years,[117]
45　　Knew many things; but when thou wert begot,
　　　Olympos[118] chimed with crystal laughter bright,
　　　Since, for thy mother, his dim vision chose
　　　A fallen statue which he deemed a nymph,
　　　White as a flint amid a field of corn.
50　　I warn thee by that memory!—thou'mistakest
　　　A prostrate stone for the fair truth of life."

　　　　Whereto the Great Unmoved no answer made,
　　　And Time continued, sterner than before.
　　　"O, not-to-be-approved! thou Apathy,
55　　Who gazest downward on that empty shell,—
　　　Is it for thee, who bear'st the common lot
　　　Of man, and art his brother in the fields,
　　　From birth to funeral pyre;[119] is it for thee,
　　　Who didst derive from thy long-living sire
60　　More knowledge than endows far better sons,—
　　　Thy lamp to burn within, and turn aside
　　　Thy face from all humanity, or behold it
　　　Without emotion, like some sea-shelled thing
　　　Staring around from a green hollowed rock,
65　　Not aiding, loving, caring—hoping aught—
　　　Forgetting nature, and by her forgot."

　　　　Whereto, with mildness, Akinetos said,
　　　"Hast thou considered of Eternity?"
　　　"Profoundly have I done so, in my youth;"
70　　Chronos[120] replied, and bowed his furrowed head;
　　　"Most, when my tender feet from Chaos trod
　　　Stumbling,—and, doubtful of my eyes, my hands
　　　The dazzling air explored. But, since that date,

---

[116] Became enamoured with Eos who asked Zeus to grant him immortality, but forgot to ask for a youthful body
[117] 180 years
[118] Musician who played wind instruments in Greek mythology
[119] Ediface for burning dead body in funeral proceeding
[120] Bodily representation of time

So many ages have I told; so many,
75 Fleet after fleet on newly opening seas,
Descry before me, that of late my thoughts
Have rather dwelt on all around my path,
With anxious care. Well were it thus with thee."

Then Akinetos calmly spake once more,
80 With eyes still bent upon the tide-ribbed sands.
"And dost thou of To-morrow also think?"
Whereat—as one dismayed by sudden thought
Of many crowding things that call him thence,—
Time, with bent brows, went hurrying on his way.

85 Slow tow'rds his cave the Great Unmoved repaired,
And, with his back against the rock, sat down
Outside, half smiling in the pleasant air;
And in the lonely silence of the place,
He thus, at length, discoursed unto himself.

90 "Orion, ever active and at work,
Honest and skilful, not to be surpassed,
Brought misery on himself and those he loved;
Caused his companions' death,—and now hath found
At Artemis's hand, his own. So fares it ever
95 With the world's builder. He, from wall to beam,
From pillar to roof, from shade to corporal form;
From the first vague Thought to the Temple vast,
A ceaseless contest with the crowd endures,
For whom he labours. Why then should we move?
100 Our wisdom cannot change whate'er's decreed,
Nor e'en the acts or thoughts of brainless men:
Why then be moved? Best reason is most vain
He who will do and suffer, must—and end.
Hence, death is not an evil, since it leads
105 To somewhat permanent, beyond the noise
Man maketh on the labor of his will,
Until the small round burst, and pale he falls.
His ear is stuffed with the grave's earth, yet feels
The inaudible whispers of Eternity,
110 While Time runs shouting to Oblivion
In the upper fields, I would not swell that cry."

Thus Akinetos sat from day to day,
Absorbed in indolent sublimity,

      Reviewing thoughts and knowledge o'er and o'er;
115 And now he spake, now sang unto himself,
      Now sank to brooding silence. From above,
      While passing, Time the rock touched!—and it oozed
      Petrific drops—gently at first—and slow.
      Reclining lonely in his fixt repose,
120 The Great Unmoved unconsciously became
      Attached to that he pressed; and soon a part
      Of the rock. There clung the excrescence,[121] till strong hands,
      Descended from Orion, made large roads,
      And built steep walls, squaring down rocks for use.
125

        When Death with moth-like wing and in-drawn breath
      Hovers above a dying brain of power,
      And the soul knows the moment of its flight
      Is surely near, there floats a crowding train
130 Of passions, thoughts, actions, events, and hopes—
      Tenderest affections, and those storms and calms
      Wherein the man each complex scene reviews,
      And in swift visions lives his course again.
      Then sigh the vain regrets o'er wasted days,
135 And wasted efforts, bred of ignorance,
      Pride, folly, vanity—or the world's gross wrongs,
      Exasperating once—now pitied. Then—
      No casuist baseness making ill acts good—
      Hurried self-questionings dart to and fro,
140 If this or that were right, or wrong—or kind,
      Mean, or magnanimous—forgiving—hard—
      Generous, or selfish;—if the sum of all,
      Balanced in fairness, were the heart's best aim?
      Nor less the painful sense of means yet strong—
145 The consciousness of so much power to do,
      And no more time for doing. How they float
      Away in mist, all those rare plans, designs—
      Clear-outlined fabrics reared on solid truths,
      Doomed to resolve themselves into the brain
150 That bred them, and be lost for evermore!
      This, and a reverent hopeful resignation,
      For many might suffice, without the fears
      Of crippled souls, that crawl to fancied hells,
      Who are mere grave-worms in reality.
155 But of his stern philosophy what thoughts
      Were last in Akinetos's mind? Said he,

---

[121] Putting on of the addition

"Annihilation means but perfect change—
All are annihilated in the end;
Or if there be no end, why that's the same,
160   If the dead know not their connecting past,
Nor present being." Held he thus to the last?
There might have been misgivings—not unwise—
That wisdom should be put to use? But he
Knew better, as he thought—and there were none.
165

Now had Poseidon with tridental spear
Torn up the smitten sea, which raged on high
With grief and anger for Orion slain;
And black Hephaestus deep beneath the earth
170   A cold thrill felt through his metallic veins,
Which soon with sparkling fire began to writhe
Like serpents, till from each volcanic peak
Burst smoke and threatening flames. Day hid his head,
And while the body of Orion sank,
175   Drawn down into the embraces of the Sea,
The four Winds with confronting fury arose,
And to a common centre drove their blasts,
Which, meeting, brake like thunder-stone, or shells
Of war, far scattering. Shipwreck fed the deep.
180   No Moon had dared the ringing vault to climb;
No star, no meteor's steed; and ancient Night
Shook the dishevelled lightning from her brows,
Then sank in deeper gloom. Ere long the roar
Rolled through a distant yawning chasm of flame,
185   Dying away, and in the air obscure,
Feverish and trembling,—like the breath of one
Recovering from convulsion's throes,—appeared
Two wavering misty shapes upon a mount:
Whence now a solemn and reproachful voice,
190   With broken pauses spake, and thus lamented.

"Call it not love!—oh never yet for thee
Did Love's ambrosial[122] pinions[123] fan the hours,
To lose themselves in bliss, which memory
195   Alone can find, so to renew their life.
Thou could'st not ever thus enjoy, thus give
Thy nature fully up; thine attributes,
Whate'er of loveliness or high estate

---

[122] Nourishing
[123] Wings

               They owned, surrendering all before Love's feet,
200   And in his breath to melt. How shall we name
               Thy passion,—ice-pure, self-entire, exacting
               All worship, for a limited return?
               But how, ah me! shall Time record the hour,
               When with thy bow—its points curved stiffly back,
205   Like a snake's neck preparing for a spring,
               Thou stood'st in lurid ire behind a cloud,
               And loosed the fatal shaft! Where then was love?
               O Artemis! O miserable Queen!
               Call it pride, jealousy, revenge—self-love;
210   No other. Thou repliest not. Wherefore pride?
               Thou gav'st thyself that wound, rejecting one
               Who to thee tendered all his nature; noble,
               Though earth-born, as thou knew'st when first ye met,
               And thou not Zeus with a creator's power
215   His being to re-make? Thou answerest not.
               Why jealous, but because thou saw'st him happy
               Without thee, though cast off by thee. Then wherefore
               Destroy? Revenge, the champion of self-love
               Can make his well-known sign. O, horrible!
220   Despair to all springs up from murdered love,
               And smites revenge with idiotcy of grief,
               Seeing itself. But wake, and look upon
               My loss unutterable. What hast thou gained?
               Nothing but anguish; and for this accomplished
225   His death, my loss, and the earth's loss beside
               Of that much-needed hand. I curse thee not—
               Thou hast, indeed, cursed me—thou know'st it well."

               With face bowed o'er her bosom, Artemis,
               As in sad trance, remained. The night was gone;
230   The day had dawned, but she perceived it not;
               Nor Eos knew that any light had passed
               From her rent robes. But hope unconsciously
               Grew up in her, and yet again she spake.

               "Ah, me! alas! why came this great affliction,
235   Which, indeed, seems beyond all remedy,
               Though scalding tears from our immortal eyes
               Make constant arcs in heaven. Beauty avails not
               Where power is needed. Seek we, then, for power,
               That some reviving or renewing beam
240   May call him back, now pale in the deep sea.

Thou answerest not. I think thou hast a heart,
Which beats thy reasoning down to silent truth,
And therefore deem I thou with me wilt seek
The throne of Zeus, who may receive our prayers,
245 Nor from our supplications, utterly
Take sorrow's sweetness, which hath secret hope,
Like honey drops in some down-fallen flower."

    Her lofty pallid visage,[124] Artemis
Raised slowly, but with eyes still downward bent
250 Upon the ocean rolling dark below,
And answered,—"I will go with thee." The twain
Departed heavily on their ascent
Through the grey air, and paused not till they reached
The region of Olympos, where their course
255 Was barriered by a mass of angry cloud
Piled up in surging blackness, with a gleam
Of smouldering red seen through at intervals.
The sign well understood, both Goddesses
Knelt down before the cloud, and Artemis
260 Brake silence first, with firm yet hollow voice.

    "Father of Gods, and of the populous earth!
Who know'st the thoughts and deeds we most would hide;
And also know'st the secret thrill within,
Which owns no thought nor action, yet comprises
265 Life's sole excuse for what seems worthiest hate—
Extremes and maddened self-opposing springs—
Not always thus excused,—O Zeus! receive
Our prayers, and chiefly mine, which pardon sue,
Besides the dear request. Grant that the life
270 Of him these hands, once dazzling white, have slain,
May be to earth restored." More had she said,
But the dark pile of cloud shook with the voice
Of Zeus, who answered: "He shall be restored;
But not returned to earth. His cycle moves
275 Ascending!" The deep sea the announcement heard;
And from beneath its ever-shifting thrones,
The murmuring of a solemn joy sent up.

    The cloud expanded darkly o'er the heavens,
Which, like a vault preparing to give back

---

[124] Appearance lacking color

280 The heroic dead, yawned with its sacred gloom,
And iron-crowned Night her black breath poured around
To meet the clouds that from Olympos rolled
Billows of darkness with a dirging roar,
Which by gradations of high harmony
285 Merged in triumphal strains. Their earnest eyes
Filled with the darkness, and their hands still clasped,
Kneeling the Goddesses bright rays perceived,
Reflected, glance before them. Mute they rose
With tender consciousness; and, hand in hand,
290 Turning, they saw slow rising from the sea
The luminous Giant clad in blazing stars,
New-born and trembling from their Maker's breath,—
Divine, refulgent effluence of Love.
Though to his insubstantial form no gleam
295 Of mortal life's rich colours now gave warmth,
Yet was the image he had worn on earth,
With all its memories of the old dim woods—
The caves—his toils, joys, griefs—the fond old ways—
The same—his heart the same, e'en as of yore.
300 With pale gold shield, like a translucent moon
Through which the morning with ascending cheek
Sheds a soft blush, warming cerulean[125] veins;
With radiant belt of glory, typical
Of happy change that o'er the zodiac round
305 Of the world's monstrous phantasies shall come;
And in his hand a sword of peaceful power,
Streaming like a meteor to direct the earth
To victory over life's distress, and shew
The future path whose light runs through death's glooms;
310 In grandeur, like the birth of Motion, rose
The glorious Giant, tow'rds his place in heaven;
And, while ascending, thus his Spirit sang.

"I came into the world a mortal creature,
Lights flitting upwards through my unwrought clay,
315 Not knowing what they were, nor whither tending,
But of some goodness conscious in my soul.
With earth's rude elements my first endeavour
I made; attained rare mastery, and was proud
Then felt strange longings in the grassy woodlands,
320 And hunted shadows under the slant sun.

---

[125] Sky blue

"O Artemis! bright queen! high benefactress!
My love forgive, that with its human feet
Could not to thy pure altitude ascend,
Nor could'st thou stoop to me. A fiery passion,
325 Deep as mortality, possessed my life;
Nor shall I from my destiny, star bright
Henceforth, and from transforming change exempt,
Banish the greatful thoughts of Merope,
Though blindness followed that ecstatic dream.

330 "On thee I gaze, blest Goddess of the Morning!
In whose sweet smile these stars shall ever melt,
All human beauty perfected in thee,
Divine with human blending. In my heart
Bared full before thee, to the essence fine
335 Wherewith, by whisperings of my Maker's breath,
These stars of my new life are now inspired—
In this pure essence shall thy treasured love
Receive my adoration; and the thoughts
Of thee shall open ever in my mind
340 Like the bland meads in flower when thou appear'st."

"Thou Earth, whom I have left, and all my brothers!
Followers of Time through steep and thorny ways;
Wrestlers with strong Calamity, and falling
For ever, as with generations new
345 Ye carry on the strife,—deem it no loss
That in full vigour of his fresh designs,
Your Worker and your Builder hath been called
To rest thus undesired. Though for himself
Too soon, and not enough of labour done
350 For high desires; sufficient yet to give
The impulse ye are fitted to receive:
More, were a vain ambition. Therefore strive,
My course, without its blindness, to pursue,
So that ye may through night, as ye behold me,
355 And also through the day by faithful hope,
Ascend to me; and he who faints half-way,
Gains yet a noble eminence o'er those
Whose feet still plod the earth with hearts o'erdusted."

360 "Then with aspiring love behold Orion!
Not for his need, but for thine own behoof:
He loved thy race, and calls thee to his side.

The human spirit is a mounting thing,
But ere it reach the constellated thrones,
365 It may attain, and on mankind bestow,
Substance, precision, mastery of hand,
Beauty intense, and power that shapes new life.
So shall each honest heart become a champion,
Each high-wrought soul a builder beyond Time—
370 The ever-hunted, ne'er o'ertaken Time,
For whom so many youthful hours are slain
Vainly: the grave's brink shews we have been deceived,
And still the aged God his flight maintains!
But not in vain the earth-born shall pursue,
375 E'en though with wayward, often stumbling feet,
That substance-bearing Shadow, if with a soul
That to an absolute unadulterate truth
Aspires, and would make active through the world,
He hath resolved to plant for future years.
380 And thus, in the end, each soul may to itself,
With truth before it as its polar guide,
Become both Time and Nature, whose fixt paths
Are spiral, and when lost will find new stars,
And in the Universal Movement join."

385   The song ceased; and at once a chorus burst
From all the stars in heaven, which now shone forth!
The Moon ascends in her 'rapt loveliness;
The Ocean swells to her forgivingly;
Bright comes the dawn, and Eos hides her face,
390 Glowing with tears divine, within the bosom
Of great Poseidon, in his rocking car
Standing erect to gaze upon his son,
Installed 'midst golden fires, which ever melt
In Eos's breath and beauty; rising still
395 With nightly brilliance, merging in the dawn,
And circling onward in eternal youth.

THE END

"Afterword"
By
Richard Henry (Hengist) Horne

Preface to "Orion: An Epic Poem in Three Books,"
Australian Edition, 1854.

"Library of the World's Best Literature, Ancient and Modern," Charles Dudley Warner, 1896, p. 7641.

Every Preface has a certain number of readers who may be described as the natural friends of Prefaces, or their natural enemies. Let me endeavour to soften the animosity of the latter by assuring them that, although this poem has gone through six or seven editions, this is the first Preface that has been written for it.

The poem of "Orion" was intended to work out a special design, applicable to all times, by means of antique or classical imagery and associations; and this design, with the hero and the several characters who appear on the scene, as well as the general structure and distribution of the action, were long considered before a line was writtten. A sort of cartoon of the whole was then made, and submitted to my friend Dr. Leonhard Schmitz, one of the most learned men of the time, and equally possessed of a profound philooophical spirit. To his kind revision and suggestions I have great pleasure in acknowledging my obligations.

Orion, the hero of my fable, is meant to present a type of the struggle of man with himself, i.e., the contest between the intellect and the senses, when the energies are equally balanced. Orion is man standing naked before Heaven and Destiny, resolved to work as a really free agent to the utmost pitch of his powers for the good of others. He is a really practical believer in his gods, and in his own conscience; a child with the strength of a giant; innocently wise; with a heart expanding towards the largeness and warmth of Nature, and a spirit unconsciously aspiring to the stars. He is a dreamer of noble dreams, and a hunter of grand shadows, all tending to healthy thought, or to practical action and structure. He is the type of a Worker and a Builder for his fellow men. He presents the picture (well or ill painted, the author cannot certainly know) of a great and simple nature, struggling to develope all its loftiest energies—determined to be, and to do, to obtain knowledge, and to use it—to live up to its faculties—feeling and acting nobly and powerfully for the service of the world, and seeking its own reward and happiness in the consciousness of a well- worked life, and the possession of a perfect sympathy enshrined in some lovely object.*

Two young poets (Charles Oilier, and George Meredith) wrote to me a few years ago their several views of the design and character of Orion, each of which was a thousand times better said than the above, and in less than half the space. I am ashamed to say that I cannot sufficiently recollect their words, or they would have stood in the place of mine.

With regard to this intense sympathy with some lovely object of passion and affection, a witty authoress once said to me—" But why should it require three goddesses to perfect one giant?" The question, though put playfully, is too profound to be answered in the same vein. I shall merely say, however, that the three great phases of the ordeal of the passion of love, which most strong natures pass through, is fairly pourtrayed in the story of "Orion." I might have represented him as finding perfection at the outset, but since the lot of humanity is seldom (if ever) so fortunate, it seemed best that he should pass through the several gradations of disappointment and suffering, in order to arrive at the highest refinement, sympathy, and happiness. If the happiness was short-lived, and met with destruction at the selfish hands of a limited nature (an imperfect sympathy), who resented the bliss it was itself incapable of attaining or conferring, that also is the type of a melancholy truth. The law of progress forbids man to rest in happiness: in his misery there is no likelyhood that he will ever rest; but this law cuts short the work of a man, not merely when he has done his best, or perhaps before, but even when he has done as much as his age is capable of using. He must go away, and make room for other greatness. The needs of a future age must be supplied by future genius.

Mr. G. H. Lewes, the author of " The History of Philosophy, &c., &c.," being a devout student of Goethe and the German metaphysicians (with whom thought is action, and action thought, i.e., they seem to regard the business of life as little more than a subject for profound speculation), endeavoured one day to show me that the real hero of my poem was not Orion, but Akinetos. Now, I had drawn the character of the giant Akinetos—the Great Unmoved—in contradistinction to that of Orion—a Great Mover of the world—the one all action, the other all thought leading to no action. If Akinetos could have heard the remark, he would have regarded it as no compliment to be called a hero of any sort: he would have asked what was the good of building houses on the sands of the ocean? The amusements of fools incapable of sitting still. The philosophy of Akinetos may be difficult to refute in the abstract, but since human life is a mixture of hard reality with perfect illusion, Akinetos was no hero, nor a good model to follow, and therefore I finally set him in a stone wall, while Orion shines for ever.

The other characters speak for themselves. My friend Alfred Tennyson, accused me on the first publication of "Orion" of intending the plausible giant Encolyon for a certain eminent statesman of the day. There was certainly an amusing resemblance in some respects; but I had no such intention. Besides, it would have been unbecoming the dignity of Epic story. While on this point, I may add that Colonel Perronet Thompson, the author of the celebrated "Corn Law Catechism," and indeed the father and prime mover of the whole of that great battle, considered that I had intended to illustrate the principles of free-trade in the episode of the inhabitants of stony Ithaca during a famine, in Canto II., Book I. I plead guilty to this, if it be a wrong in the eyes of the Epic Muse; but while I believe the principles there imagined in fable to be simple and universal—applicable in all ages—I trust the form and picture are sufficiently idealized to be in perfect harmony with the rest of the story, its local scenery and characteristics. The reader, therefore, ought not, I think, to reproach me for this, especially as it is not certain that many people would have found it out, if I had not told them.

Of the design and structure of this Poem, as a work of imagination, it does not become me to speak; but as various remarks were made in England on its philosophy, to which I never offered any reply, a few words may now, for the first time, be given in explanation.

The philosophy of "Orion" gives the widest scope to nature, natural action, and genius; it advocates the broadest views, and most energetic progress, with a belief in the constant advancement of mankind, here and hereafter. It may be said that the converse of this picture can be shown by the quotation of certain passages; and the words of the starving man gathering gum from the lentisk-trees, have been cited,—

> Like the hot springs
> That boil themselves away, and serve for nought,
> Which yet must have some office, rightly used,
> Man hath a secret source for some great end,
> Which by delay seems wasted. Ignorance
> Clokes us, and Time outwits us. —Book I., Canto III.

This is admitted; nor need I be ashamed to confess that I have myself had hours, even days, of extreme despondency, during which the foregoing lines were realized to a degree that had I then been dying might have induced me to choose those words for my epitaph. But that is no proof. With all vigorous natures these periods of gloom and hopelessness are very brief; and for every single passage of such tendency in " Orion," a dozen may be found of the opposite; and this belief in the progress of man is expressly developed in the opening of Book III., Canto I. Although it may be true in some rare instances that,—

> The man, who for his race might supersede
> The work of ages, dies worn out—not used!
> Yet it is shown that his influence continues—
> The circle widens as the world spins round-
> The earth hath tough rind,but a subtle heart-
> His soul works on,while he sleeps 'neath the grass.

The opening of the last Canto, and the concluding Song of Orion, after death, while taking his place among the constellated thrones, certainly place the philosophy of the poem beyond question as a whole, whatever speeches or remarks may be cited from Akinetos.

With similar design, the Intellectual and the Sensuous have each been given a fair and open field. Detached passages might be found equally forcible on both sides; and in order not to put forth any equivocating philosphy on this point, a certain sage gives an opinion in opposition to all the courtiers of Oinopion's palace,—

> That human nerves,
> And what they wrought, were wondrous as the mind,
> And, in the eye of Zeus, none could decide
> Which held the higher place. —Book II., Canto I.

Yet the direct tendency of the fable, as far as it relates to the passion of love, is clearly shown to advocate that combination of the intellectual and the sensuous, which is most conducive to the noble progress and happiness of special natures.

In like manner, when a critic in the "Athenaeum" designated "Orion" as a "spiritual epic" he might with equal truth have termed it a corporeal epic, or one of mere external action. It is both. The life of Orion began amidst "ponderous substance," and is continually employed in physical action, when not absorbed with the converse. The poem is intended equally to advocate the real and the ideal, the precursive dream, theory, or shadow—and the substance and action which they originate.

I have been very frequently requested, particularly by letters from total strangers, to make some explanations of this kind concerning the design of "Orion," and have always resisted, simply because it seemed to me that it was plain enough, or at least open to such study as any epic poem, at all worthy of the name, might fairly ask of all lovers of poetry. I trust, however, that my tardy consent will not have made any of my old readers, in various parts of the world, angry or indifferent, since I have ever regarded an intellectual sympathy as the highest treasure an author can obtain, the only heartfelt reward of all his labors.

In the early editions there stood, instead of Preface, the following Note:—

> "I have adopted the Greek mythological names throughout this poem, with a view of getting rid of commonizing associations. It has become an arduous, if not impossible task for the popular imagination to rise up to the purely

poetic conception of such abstractions as a Juno, a Neptune, a Diana, amidst all the perverting associations with which they are now surrounded. As to such a change being more correct in writing from an old Greek fable, there can hardly be two opinions. The gods and goddesses of ancient Italy were perfectly distinct from those of ancient Greece, although certain prominent attributes existed in common between the Jupiter of the Romans, and Zeus of the Greeks; between Diana and Artemis; between Vulcan, and Hephsestos; Neptune and Poseidon, &c. It has been my object to create.new associations, founded upon those of the antique age which are the most purely poetical and suggestive. With this view, the names are of no great importance to those who do not recognize them classically, and I trust that my fable would be perfectly intelligible to all classes of readers, by whatever names the characters were designated. Meantime, the design of this poem of " Orion" is far from being intended as a mere echo or reflection of the Past, and is in itself, and in other respects, a novel experiment upon the mind of a nation."

With this view, as there was scarcely any instance of an Epic Poem attaining any popular circulation during its author's life time, the first three editions were given gratuitously—that is, they were published at a nominal price, which amounted to the same thing as a gift; but the circulation by no means diminished upon each of the subsequent editions. The last edition has now been out of print some two years and a half; in fact before I sailed for Australia, about which time a republication of the Poem was in contemplation. I little imagined on leaving England that the next edition of "Orion" as an "experiment upon the mind of a nation" (in embryo, though this nation is) would be called for in Melbourne. It is with difficulty, even now, in writing this Preface, that I can realize the fact with the barren "bush" around me, and so entire a change in my associations,—indeed I do not at all feel as if I had written the work.

Review of "Orion"
By
Edgar Allan Poe
Graham's Magazine, March 1844

Edgar Allan Poe

In the January number of this magazine, the receipt of this work was mentioned, and it was hinted that, at some future period, it should be made the subject of review. We proceed now to fulfill that promise.

And first a word or two of gossip and personality.

Mr. R. H. Horne, the author of "Orion," has, of late years, acquired a high and extensive *home* reputation, although, as yet, he is only partially known in America. He will be remembered, however, as the author of a very well-written Intro-duction to Black's Translation of Schlegel's "Lectures on Dramatic Art and Literature," and as a contributor with Wordsworth, Hunt, Miss Barrett, and others, to "Chaucer Modernized." He is the author, also, of "Cosmo de Medici," of "The Death of Marlowe," and, especially, of "Gregory the Seventh," a fine tragedy, prefaced with an "Essay on Tragic Influence." "Orion" was originally advertised to be sold for *a farthing*; and, at this price, three large editions were actually sold. The fourth edition, (a specimen of which now lies before us) was issued at a shilling, and also *sold*. A fifth is promised at half a crown; this likewise, with even a sixth at a crown, may be disposed of — partly through the intrinsic merit of the work itself — but, chiefly, through the ingenious novelty of the original price.

We have been among the earliest readers of Mr. Horne among the most earnest admirers of his high genius; — for a man of high, of the highest genius, he unquestionably is. With an eager wish to do justice to his "Gregory the Seventh," we have never yet found exactly that opportunity we desired. Meantime, we looked, with curiosity, for what the British critics would say of a work which, in the boldness of its conception, and in the fresh originality of its management, would necessarily fall beyond the *routine* of their customary verbiage. We saw nothing, however, that either could or should be understood — nothing, certainly, that was worth understanding. The tragedy itself was, unhappily, not devoid of the ruling cant of the day, and its critics (that cant incarnate) took their cue from some of its infected passages, and proceeded forthwith to rhapsody and Æsthetics, by way of giving a common-sense public an intelligible idea of the book. By the "cant of the day" we mean the disgusting practice of putting on the airs of an owl, and endeavoring to look miraculously wise; — the affectation of second sight — of a species of ecstatic prescience — of an intensely bathetic penetration into all sorts of mysteries, psychological ones in especial; — an Orphic — an ostrich affectation, which buries its head in balderdash, and, seeing nothing itself, fancies, therefore, that its preposterous carcass is not a visible object of derision for the world at large.

Of "Orion" itself, we have, as yet, seen few notices in the British periodicals, and these few are merely repetitions of the old jargon. All that has been said, for example, might be summed up in some such paragraph as this:

"'Orion' is the *earnest* outpouring of the oneness of the psychological Man. It has the individuality of the true Singleness. It is not to be regarded as a Poem, but as a Work — as a multiple Theogony — as a manifestation of the Works and the Days. It is a pinion in the Progress — a wheel in the Movement that moveth ever and goeth alway a mirror of Self-Inspection, held up by the Seer of the Age essential — of the Age *in esse* — for the Seers of the Ages possible — *in posse*. We hail a brother in the work."

Of the mere opinions of the donkeys who bray thus — of their mere dogmas and doctrines, literary, Æsthetical, or what not — we know little, and, upon our honor, we wish to know less.

Occupied, Laputically, in their great work of a progress that never progresses, we take it for granted, also, that they care as little about ours. But whatever the opinions of these people may be — however portentous the "Idea" which they have been so long threatening to "evolve" — we still think it clear that they take a very roundabout way of evolving it. The use of Language is in the promulgation of Thought. If a man — if an Orphicist — or a Seer — or whatever else he may choose to call himself, while the rest of the world calls him an ass — if this gentleman have an idea which he does not understand himself, the best thing he can do is to say nothing about it; for, of course, he can entertain no hope that what he, the Seer, cannot comprehend, should be comprehended by the mass of common humanity; but if he have an idea which is actually intelligible to himself, and if he sincerely wish to render it intelligible to others, we then hold it as indisputable that he should employ those forms of speech which are the best adapted to further his object. He should speak to the people in that people's ordinary tongue. He should arrange words, such as are habitually employed for the several preliminary and introductory ideas to be conveyed he should arrange them in collocations such as those in which we are accustomed to see those words arranged.

But to all this the Orphicist thus replies: "I am a Seer. My Idea — the idea which by Providence I am especially commissioned to evolve — is one so vast — so novel — that ordinary words, in ordinary collocations, will be insufficient for its comfortable evolution." Very true. We grant the vastness of the Idea — it is manifested in the sucking of the thumb — but, then, if *ordinary* language be insufficient — the ordinary language which men understand — *à fortiori* will be insufficient that inordinate language which no man has *ever* understood, and which any well-educated baboon would blush in being accused of understanding. The "Seer," therefore, has no resource but to oblige mankind by holding his tongue, and suffering his Idea to remain quietly "unevolved," until some Mesmeric mode of intercommunication shall be invented, whereby the antipodal brains of the Seer and of the man of Common Sense shall be brought into the necessary *rapport*. Meantime we earnestly ask if *bread-and-butter* be the vast Idea in question — if *bread-and-butter* be any portion of this vast Idea; for we have often observed that when a Seer has to speak of even so usual a thing as bread-and-butter, he can never be induced to mention it outright. He will, if you choose, say any thing and every thing *but* bread-and-butter. He will consent to hint at buckwheat cake. He may even accommodate you so far as to insinuate oatmeal porridge — but, if bread-and-butter be really the matter intended, we never yet met the Orphicist who could get out the three individual words "bread-and-butter."

We have already said that "Gregory the Seventh" was, unhappily, infected with the customary cant of the day — the cant of the muddle-pates who dishonor a profound and ennobling philosophy by styling themselves transcendentalists. In fact, there are few highly sensitive or imaginative intellects for which the vortex of *mysticism*, in any shape, has not an almost irresistible influence, on account of the shadowy confines which separate the Unknown from the Sublime. Mr. Horne, then, is, in some measure, infected. The success of his previous works had led him to attempt, zealously, the production of a poem which should be worthy his high powers. We have no doubt that he revolved carefully in mind a variety of august conceptions, and from these thoughtfully selected what his judgment, rather than what his impulses, designated as the noblest and the best. In a word, he has weakly yielded his own poetic sentiment of the poetic — yielded it, in some degree, to the pertinacious opinion, and *talk*, of a certain junto by which he is surrounded — a junto of dreamers whose absolute intellect may, perhaps, compare with his own very much after the fashion of an ant-hill with the Andes. By this talk — by its continuity rather than by any other quality it possessed — he has been badgered into the attempt at commingling the obstinate oils and waters of Poetry and of Truth. He has been so far blinded as to permit himself to imagine that a maudlin philosophy (granting it to be worth enforcing) could be enforced by poetic imagery, and illustrated by the jingling of rhythm; or, more unpardonably, he has been induced to believe that a poem, whose single object is the creation of Beauty — the novel collocation of old forms of the Beautiful and of the Sublime — could be advanced by the abstractions of a maudlin philosophy.

But the question is not even this. It is not whether it be not possible to introduce didacticism, with effect, into a poem, or possible to introduce poetical images and measures, with effect, into a didactic essay. To do either the one or the other, would be merely to surmount a difficulty — would be simply a feat of literary sleight of hand. But the true question is, whether the author who shall attempt either feat, will not be laboring at a disadvantage — will not be guilty of a fruitless and wasteful expenditure of energy. In minor poetical efforts, we may not so imperatively demand an adherence to the true poetical thesis. We permit *trifling* to some extent, in a work which we consider a trifle at best. Although we agree, for example, with Coleridge, that poetry and *passion* are discordant, yet we are willing to permit Tennyson to bring, to the intense *passion* which prompted his "Locksley Hall," the aid of that terseness and pungency which are derivable from rhythm and from rhyme. The effect he produces, however, is a purely passionate, and not, unless in detached passages of this magnificent philippic, a properly poetic effect. His "Œnone," on the other hand, exalts the soul not into passion, but into a conception of pure *beauty*, which in its elevation its calm and intense rapture — has in it a foreshadowing of the future and spiritual life, and as far transcends earthly passion as the holy radiance of the sun does the glimmering and feeble phosphorescence of the glow-worm. His "Morte D'Arthur" is in the same majestic vein. The "Sensitive Plant" of Shelley is in the same sublime spirit. Nor, if the passionate poems of Byron excite more intensely a greater number of readers than either the "Œnone" or the "Sensitive Plant" does this indisputable fact prove any thing more than that the majority of mankind are more susceptible of the impulses of passion than of the impressions of beauty. Readers do exist, however, and always will exist, who, to hearts of maddening fervor, unite, in perfection, the sentiment of the beautiful that divine sixth sense which is yet so faintly understood that sense which phrenology has attempted to embody in its organ of *ideality* — that sense which is the basis of all Fourier's dreams — that sense which speaks of God through his purest, if not his *sole* attribute — which proves, and which alone proves his existence.

To readers such as these — and only to such as these — must be left the decision of what the true Poesy is. And these with *no* hesitation — will decide that the origin of Poetry lies in a thirst for a wilder Beauty than Earth supplies — that Poetry itself is the imperfect effort to quench this immortal thirst by novel combinations of beautiful forms (collocations of forms) physical or spiritual, and that this thirst when even partially allayed — this sentiment when even feebly meeting response — produces emotion to which all other human emotions are vapid and insignificant.

We shall now be fully understood. If, with Coleridge, who, however erring at times, was precisely the mind fitted to decide a question such as this — if, with him, we reject *passion* from the true — from the pure poetry — if we reject even passion — if we discard as feeble, as unworthy the high spirituality of the theme, (which has its origin in a sense of the Godhead) if we dismiss even the nearly divine emotion of human *love* — that emotion which, merely to name, *now* causes the pen to tremble — with how much greater reason shall we dismiss all else? And yet there are men who would mingle with the august theme the merest questions of expediency — the cant topics of the day — the doggerel Æsthetics of the time — who would trammel the soul in its flight to an ideal Helusion, by the quirks and quibbles of chopped logic. There are men who do this lately there are a set of men who make a practice of doing this — and who defend it on the score of the advancement of what they suppose to be *truth*. Truth is, in its own essence, sub-lime — but her loftiest sublimity, as derived from man's clouded and erratic reason, is valueless — is pulseless — is utterly ineffective when brought into comparison with the unerring *sense* of which we speak; yet grant this *truth* to be all which its seekers and worshipers pretend — they forget that it is not truth, *per se*, which is made their thesis, but an *argumentation*, often maudlin and pedantic, always shallow and unsatisfactory (as from the mere inadaptation of the vehicle it *must* be) by which this *truth*, in casual and indeterminate glimpses, is *or is not* — rendered manifest.

We have said that, in minor poetical efforts, we may tolerate some deflection from the true poetical thesis; but when a man of the highest powers sets himself seriously to the task of constructing what shall be most worthy those powers, we expect that he shall so choose his theme as to render it certain that he labor not at disadvantage. We regret to see any trivial or partial imperfection of detail; but we grieve deeply when we detect any radical error of conception.

In setting about "Orion," Mr. Horne proposed to himself, (in accordance with the views of his junto) to "elaborate a morality" — he ostensibly proposed this to himself — for, in the depths of his heart, we *know* that he wished all juntos and all moralities in Erebus. In accordance with the notions of his *set*, however, he felt a species of shame-facedness in not making the enforcement of some certain dogmas or doctrines (questionable or unquestionable) about Progress, the obvious or apparent object of his poem. This shame-facedness is the cue to the concluding sentence of the Preface. "Mean time, the design of this poem of

'Orion' is far from being intended as a mere echo or reflection of the past, and is, in itself, and in other respects, a novel experiment upon the mind of a nation." Mr. Horne conceived, in fact, that to compose a poem merely for that poem's sake — and to acknowledge such to be his purpose — would be to subject himself to the charge of imbecility — of triviality — of deficiency in the true dignity and force; but, had he listened to the dictates of his own soul, he could not have failed to perceive, at once, that under the sun there exists no work more intrinsically noble, than this very poem *written solely for the poem's sake.*

But let us regard "Orion" as it is. It has an under and an upper current of meaning; in other words, it is an allegory. But the poet's sense of fitness (which, under no circumstances of mere conventional opinion, could be more than half subdued) has so far softened this allegory as to keep it, generally, well subject to the ostensible narrative. The purport of the moral conveyed is by no means clear — showing conclusively that the heart of the poet was not with it. It vacillates. At one time a certain set of opinions predominate — then another. We may generalize the subject, however, by calling it a homily against supineness or apathy in the cause of human progress, and in favor of energetic action for the good of the race. This is precisely *the* idea of the present school of canters. How feebly the case is made out in the poem — how insufficient has been all Mr. Horne's poetical rhetoric in convincing even himself — may be gleaned from the unusual bombast, rigmarole, and mystification of the concluding paragraph, in which he has thought it necessary to say something *very* profound, by way of putting the sting to his epigram, the point to his moral. The words put us much in mind of the "nonsense verses" of Du Bartas.

> And thus, in the end, each soul may to itself,
> With truth before it as its polar guide,
> Become both Time and Nature, whose fixt paths
> Are spiral, and when lost will find new stars,
> And in the universal Movement join.

The upper current of the theme is based upon the various Greek fables about Orion. The author, in his brief preface, speaks about "writing from an old Greek fable" — but his story is, more properly, a very judicious selection and modification of a great variety of Greek and Roman fables concerning Orion and other personages with whom these fables bring Orion in collision. And here we have only to object that the really magnificent abilities of Mr. Horne might have been better employed in an entirely original conception. The story he tells is beautiful indeed, — and *nil tetigit*, certainly, *quod non ornavit* — but our memories — our classic recollections are continually at war with his claims to regard, and we too often find ourselves rather speculating upon what he might have done, than admiring what he has really accomplished.

The narrative, as our poet has arranged it, runs nearly thus: Orion, hunting on foot amid the mountains of Chios, encounters Artemis (Diana) with her train. The goddess, at first indignant at the giant's intrusion upon her grounds, becomes, in the second place, enamored. Her pure love spiritualizes the merely animal nature of Orion, but does not render him happy. He is filled with vague aspirations and desires. He buries himself in sensual pleasures. In the mad dreams of intoxication, he beholds a vision of Merope, the daughter of Œnopion, king of Chios. She is the type of physical beauty. She cries in his ear, "Depart from Artemis! She loves thee not — thou art too full of earth." Awaking, he seeks the love of Merope. It is returned. Œnopion, dreading the giant and his brethren, yet scorning his pretensions, temporizes. He consents to bestow upon Orion the hand of Merope, on condition of the island being cleared, within six days, of its savage beasts and serpents. Orion, seeking the aid of his brethren, accomplishes the task. Œnopion again hesitates. Enraged, the giants make war upon him, and carry off the princess. In a remote grove Orion lives, in bliss, with his earthly love. From this delirium of happiness, he is aroused by the vengeance of Œnopion, who causes him to be surprised while asleep, and deprived of sight. The princess, being retaken, immediately forgets and deserts her lover, who, in his wretchedness, seeks, at the suggestion of a shepherd, the aid of Eos (Aurora) who, also becoming enamored of him, restores his sight. The love of Eos, less earthly than that of Merope, less cold than that of Artemis, fully satisfies his soul. He is at length happy. But the jealousy of Artemis destroys him. She pierces him with her arrows while in the very act of gratefully renovating her temple at Delos. In despair, Eos flies to Artemis, reproves her, represents to her the bareness of her jealousy and revenge, softens her, and obtains her consent to unite with herself — with Eos — in a prayer to Zeus (Jupiter) for the restoration of the giant to life. The prayer is heard. Orion is not only restored to life, but rendered immortal, and placed among the constellations, where he enjoys forever the pure affection of Eos, and becomes extinguished, each morning, in her rays.

In ancient mythology, the giants are meant to typify various energies of Nature. Pursuing, we suppose, this idea, Mr. Horne has made his own giants represent certain principles of human action or passion. Thus Orion himself is the Worker or Builder, and is the type of Action or Movement itself — but, in various portions of the poem, this allegorical character is left out of sight, and that of speculative philosophy takes its place; a mere consequence of the general uncertainty of purpose, which is the chief defect of the work. Sometimes we even find Orion a Destroyer in place of a Builder up — as, for example, when he destroys the grove about the temple of Artemis, at Delos. Here he usurps the proper allegorical attribute of Rhexergon, (the second of the seven giants named) who is the Breaker-down, typifying the Revolutionary Principle. Autarces, the third, represents the Mob, or, more strictly, Waywardness — Capricious Action. Harpax, the fourth, serves for Rapine — Briastor, the fifth, for Brute Force — Encolyon, the sixth, the "Chainer of the Wheel," for Conservatism — and Akinetos, the seventh, and most elaborated, for Apathy. He is termed "The Great Unmoved," and in his mouth is put all the "worldly wisdom," or selfishness, of the tale. The philosophy of Akinetos is, that no merely human exertion has any appreciable effect upon the *Movement*; and it is amusing to perceive how this great *Truth* (for most sincerely do we hold it to be such) speaks out from the real heart of the poet, through his Akinetos, in spite of all endeavor to overthrow it by the ex-ample of the brighter fate of Orion.

The death of Akinetos is a singularly forcible and poetic conception, and will serve to show how the giants are made to perish, generally, during the story, in agreement with their allegorical natures. The "Great Unmoved" quietly seats himself in a cave after the death of all his brethren, except Orion.

> Thus Akinetos sat from day to day,
> Absorbed in indolent sublimity,
> Reviewing thoughts and knowledge o'er and o'er;
> And now he spake, now sang unto himself,
> Now sank to brooding silence. From above,
> While passing, Time the rock touch'd, and it oozed
> Petrific drops — gently at first and slow.
> Reclining lonely in his fixed repose,
> The Great Unmoved unconsciously became
> Attached to that he pressed; and soon a part

Of the rock. *There clung th' excrescence, till strong hands,*
Descended from Orion, made large roads,
And built steep walls, squaring down rocks for use.

The italicized conclusion of this fine passage affords an instance, however, of a very blameable concision, too much affected throughout the poem.

In the deaths of Autarces, Harpax, and Encolyon, we recognize the same exceeding vigor of conception. These giants conspire against Orion, who seeks the aid of Artemis, who, in her turn, seeks the assistance of Phoibos (Phœbus.) The conspirators are in a cave, with Orion.

> Now Phoibos thro' the cave
> Sent a broad ray! and lo! the solar beam
> Filled the great cave with radiance equable
> And not a cranny held one speck of shade.
> A moony halo round Orion came,
> As of some pure protecting influence,
> While with intense light glared the walls and roof,
> The heat increasing. The three giants stood
> With glazing eyes, fixed. Terribly the light
> Beat on the dazzled stone, and the cave hummed
> With reddening heat, till the red hair and beard
> Of Harpax showed no difference from the rest,
> Which once were iron-black. The sullen walls
> Then smouldered down to steady oven heat,
> Like that with care attain'd when bread has ceased
> Its steaming and displays an angry tan.
> The appalled faces of the giants showed
> Full consciousness of their immediate doom.
> And soon the cave a potter's furnace glow'd
> Or kiln for largest bricks, and thus remained
> The while Orion, in his halo clasped
> By some invisible power, beheld the clay
> Of these his early friends change. Life was gone.
> Now sank the heat — the cave-walls lost their glare,
> The red lights faded, and the halo pale
> Around him, into chilly air expanded.
> There stood the three great images, in hue
> Of chalky white and red, like those strange shapes
> In Egypt's ancient tombs; but presently
> Each visage and each form with cracks and flaws

> Was seamed, and the lost countenance brake up,
> As, with brief toppling, forward prone they fell.

The deaths of Rhexergon and Biastor seem to discard (and this we regret not) the allegorical meaning altogether, but are related with even more exquisite richness and delicacy of imagination, than even those of the other giants. Upon this occasion it is the *jealousy* of Artemis which destroys.

> —But with the eve Fatigue o'ercame the giants, and they slept.
> Dense were the rolling clouds, starless the glooms;
> But o'er a narrow rift, once drawn apart,
> Showing a field remote of violet hue,
> The high Moon floated, and her downward gleam
> Shone on the upturned giant faces. Rigid
> Each upper feature, loose the nether jaw;
> Their arms cast wide with open palms; their chests
> Heaving like some large engine. Near them lay
> Their bloody clubs, with dust and hair begrimed,
> Their spears and girdles, and the long-noosed thongs.
> Artemis vanished; all again was dark.
> With day's first streak Orion rose, and loudly
> To his companions called. But still they slept.
> Again he shouted; yet no limb they stirr'd,
> Tho' scarcely seven strides distant. He approached,
> *And found the spot, so sweet with clover flower*
> *When they had cast them down, was now arrayed*
> *With many-headed poppies, like a crowd*
> *Of dusky Ethiops in a magic cirque*
> *Which had sprung up beneath them in the night.*
> *And all entranced the air.*

There are several minor defects in "Orion," and we may as well mention them here. We sometimes meet with an instance of bad taste in a revolting picture or image; for example, at page 59, of this edition:

> Naught fearing, swift, brimfull of raging life,
> *Stiff'ning they lay in pools of jellied gore.*

Sometimes — indeed very often — we encounter an altogether purposeless oddness or foreignness of speech. For example, at page 78[69]:

> As in Dodona once, ere driven thence
> By Zeus *for that* Rhexergon burnt some oaks.

Mr. Horne will find it impossible to assign a good reason for not here using "because."

Pure *vaguenesses* of speech abound. For example, page 89[79]:

> — one central heart wherein
> Time beats twin pulses with Humanity.

Now and then sentences are rendered needlessly obscure through mere involution — as at page 103[87]:

> Star-rays that first played o'er my blinded orbs,
> E'en as they glance above the lids of sleep,
> Who else had never known surprise, nor hope,
> Nor useful action.

Here the "who" has no grammatical antecedent, and would naturally be referred to sleep; whereas it is intended for "me," understood, or involved, in the pronoun "my;" as if the sentence were written thus — "rays that first played o'er the blinded orbs of me, who &c." It is useless to dwell upon so pure an affectation.
The versification throughout is, generally, of a very remarkable excellence. At times, however, it is rough, to no purpose; as at page 44[47]:

> And ever tended to some central point
> *In some place — nought more could I understand.*

And here, at page 81[71]:

> The shadow of a stag stoops to the stream
> *Swift rolling toward the cataract and drinks deeply.*

The above is an unintentional and false Alexandrine — including a foot too much, and that a trochee in place of an iambus. But here, at page 106[92], we have the utterly unjustifiable anomaly of half a foot too little:

> *And Eos ever rises circling*
> The varied regions of Mankind, &c.

All these are mere inadvertences, of course; for the general handling of the rhythm shows the profound metrical sense of the poet. He is, perhaps, somewhat too fond of "making the sound an echo to the sense." "Orion" embodies some of the most remarkable instances of this on record; but if smoothness — if the true rhythm of a verse be sacrificed, the sacrifice is an error. The effect is only a beauty, we think, where *no* sacrifice is made in its behalf. It will be found possible to reconcile *all* the objects in view. Nothing can justify such lines as this, at page 69[63]:

As snake-songs midst stone hollows thus has taught me.

We might urge, as another minor objection, that all the giants are made to speak in the same manner — with the same phraseology. Their characters are broadly distinctive, while their words are identical in spirit. There is sufficient individuality of sentiment, but little, or none, of language.

We *must* object, too, to the personal and political allusions — to the Corn-Law question, for example — to Wellington's statue, &c. These things, *of course*, have no business in a poem.

We will conclude our fault-finding with the remark that, as a consequence of the one radical error of conception upon which we have commented at length, the reader's attention, throughout, is painfully *diverted*. He is always pausing, amid poetical beauties, in the expectation of detecting among them some philosophical, allegorical moral. Of course, he does not fully, because he cannot uniquely, appreciate the beauties. The absolute necessity of re-perusing the poem, in order thoroughly to comprehend it, is also, most surely, to be regretted, and arises, likewise, from the one radical sin.

But of the *beauties* of this most remarkable poem, what shall we say? And here we find it a difficult task to be calm. And yet we have never been accused of enthusiastic encomium. It is our deliberate opinion that, in all that regards the loftiest and holiest attributes of the true Poetry, "Orion" has *never* been excelled. Indeed we feel strongly inclined to say that it has never been *equaled*. Its imagination — that quality which is all in all — is of the most refined — the most elevating — the most august character. And here we deeply regret that the necessary limits of this review will prevent us from entering, at length, into specification. In reading the poem, we marked passage after passage for extract — but, in the end, we found that we had marked nearly every passage in the book. We can now do nothing more than select a few. This, from page 3[16], introduces Orion himself, and we quote it, not only as an instance of refined and picturesque imagination, but as evincing the high artistical skill with which a scholar in spirit can paint an elaborate picture by a few brief touches.

> The scene in front two sloping mountains' sides
> Display'd; in shadow one and one in light.
> The loftiest on its summit now sustained
> The sun-beams, raying like a mighty wheel
> Half seen, which left the forward surface dark
> In its full breadth of shade; the coming sun
> Hidden as yet behind: the other mount,
> Slanting transverse, swept with an eastward face
> Catching the golden light. Now while the peal
> Of the ascending chase told that the rout
> Still midway rent the thickets, suddenly
> Along the broad and sunny slope appeared
> *The shadow of a stag that fled across*
> *Followed by a giant's shadow with a spear.*

These shadows are those of the coming Orion and his game. But who can fail to appreciate the intense beauty of the heralding shadows? Nor is this all. This "Hunter of shadows, he himself a shade," is made symbolical, or suggestive, throughout the poem, of the speculative character of Orion; and occasionally, of his pursuit of visionary happiness. For example, at page 81[71], Orion, possessed of Merope, dwells with her in a remote and dense grove of cedars. Instead of directly describing his attained happiness — his perfected bliss — the poet, with an exalted sense of Art, *for which we look utterly in vain in any other poem*, merely introduces the image of the tamed or subdued *shadow-stag*, quietly browsing and drinking beneath the cedars.

> There, underneath the boughs, mark where the gleam
> Of sun-rise thro' the roofing's chasm is thrown
> Upon a grassy plot below, whereon
> The shadow of a stag stoops to the stream,
> Swift rolling toward the cataract, and drinks.
> Throughout the day unceasingly it drinks,
> While ever and anon the nightingale,
> Not waiting for the evening, swells his hymn —
> His one sustained and heaven aspiring tone —

> And when the sun hath vanished utterly,
> Arm over arm the cedars spread their shade,
> With arching wrist and long extended hands,
> And grave-ward fingers lengthening in the moon,
> Above that shadowy stag whose antlers still
> Hung o'er the stream.

There is nothing more richly — more weirdly — more chastely — more sublimely imaginative — in the wide realm of poetical literature. It will be seen that we *have* enthusiasm but we reserve it for pictures such as this.

At page 62[58], Orion, his brethren dead, is engaged alone in extirpating the beasts from Chios. In the passages we quote, observe, in the beginning, the singular *lucidness* of detail; the arrangement of the barriers, &c., by which the hunter accomplishes his purpose, is given in a dozen lines of verse, with far more perspicuity than ordinary writers could give it in as many pages of prose. In this species of narration Mr. Horne is approached only by Moore in his "Alciphron." In the latter portions of our extract, observe the vivid picturesqueness of the description.

> Four days remain. Fresh trees he felled and wove
> More barriers and fences; inaccessible
> To fiercest charge of droves, and to o'erleap
> Impossible. These walls he so arranged
> That to a common centre each should force
> The flight of those pursued; and from that centre
> Diverged three outlets. One, the wide expanse
> Which from the rocks and inland forests led;
> One was the clear-skied windy gap above
> A precipice; the third, a long ravine
> Which through steep slopes, down to the seashore ran
> Winding, and then direct into the sea.
> Two days remain. Orion, in each hand
> Waving a torch, his course at night began,
> Through wildest haunts and lairs of savage beasts.
> With long-drawn howl, before him trooped the wolves —
> The panthers, terror-stricken, and the bears
> With wonder and gruff rage; from desolate crags,
> Leering hyenas, griffin, hippogrif,
> Skulked, or sprang madly, as the tossing brands
> Flashed through the midnight nooks and hollows cold,

Sudden as fire from flint; o'er crashing thickets,
With crouched head and curled fangs dashed the wild boar,
Gnashing forth on with reckless impulses,
While the clear-purposed fox crept closely down
Into the underwood, to let the storm,
Whate'er its cause, pass over. Through dark fens,
Marshes, green rushy swamps, and margins reedy,
Orion held his way — and rolling shapes
Of serpent and of dragon moved before him
With high-reared crests, swan-like yet terrible,
And often looking back with gem-like eyes.
All night Orion urged his rapid course
In the vex'd rear of the swift-droving din,
And when the dawn had peered, the monsters all
Were hemmed in barriers. These he now o'erheaped
With fuel through the day, and when again
Night darkened, and the sea a gulf-like voice
Sent forth, the barriers at all points he fired,
Mid prayers to HephÆstos and his Ocean-Sire.
Soon as the flames had eaten out a gap
In the great barrier fronting the ravine
That ran down to the sea, Orion grasped
Two blazing boughs; one high in air he raised,
The other, *with its roaring foliage trailed*
Behind him as he sped. Onward the droves
Of frantic creatures with one impulse rolled
Before this night-devouring thing of flames,
With multitudinous voice and downward sweep
Into the sea, which now first knew a tide,
And, ere they made one effort to regain
The shore, had caught them in its flowing arms,
And bore them past all hope. The living mass,
Dark heaving o'er the waves resistlessly,
At length, in distance, seemed a circle small,
Midst which one creature in the centre rose,
Conspicuous in the long, red quivering gleams
That from the dying brands streamed o'er the waves.
It was the oldest dragon of the fens,
Whose forky flag-wings and horn-crested head
O'er crags and marshes regal sway had held;
And now he rose up like an embodied curse,
From all the doomed, fast sinking — some just sunk —
Looked landward o'er the sea, and flapped his vans,
Until Poseidon drew them swirling down.

Poseidon (Neptune) is Orion's father, and lends him his aid. The first line italized is an example of sound made echo to sense. The rest we have merely emphasized as peculiarly imaginative.

At page 9[20], Orion thus describes a palace built by him for HephÆstos (Vulcan.)

> But, ere a shadow-hunter I became —
> A dreamer of strange dreams by day and night —
> For him I built a palace underground,
> Of iron, black and rough as his own hands.
> Deep in the groaning disemboweled earth,
> The tower-broad pillars and huge stanchions,
> And slant supporting wedges I set up,
> Aided by the Cyclops who obeyed my voice,
> *Which through the metal fabric rang and pealed*
> *In orders echoing far, like thunder-dreams.*
> With arches, galleries and domes all carved —
> *So that great figures started from the roof*
> *And lofty coignes, or sat and downward gazed*
> *On those who strode below and gazed above —*
> I filled it; in the centre framed a hall:
> Central in that, a throne; *and for the light,*
> *Forged mighty hammers that should rise and fall*
> *On slanted rocks of granite and of flint,*
> *Worked by a torrent, for whose passage down*
> *A chasm I hewed. And here the god could take,*
> *Midst showery sparks and swathes of broad gold fire*
> *His lone repose, lulled by the sounds he loved;*
> *Or, casting back the hammer-heads till they choked*
> *The water's course, enjoy, if so he wished,*
> *Midnight tremendous, silence, and iron sleep.*

The description of the Hell in "Paradise Lost" is *altogether inferior* in graphic effect, in originality, in expression, in the true imagination — to these magnificent — to these unparalleled passages. For this assertion there are tens of thousands who will condemn us as heretical; but there are a "chosen few" who will feel, in their inmost souls, the simple truth of the assertion. The former class would at least be silent, could they form even a remote conception of *that* contempt with which we hearken to their conventional jargon.

We have room for no farther extracts of length; but we refer the reader who shall be so fortunate as to procure a copy of "Orion," to a passage at page 22[30], commencing:

> One day at noontide, when the chase was done.

It is descriptive of a group of lolling hounds, intermingled with sylvans, fawns, nymphs and oceanides. We refer him also to page 25[32], where Orion, enamored of the naked beauty of Artemis, is repulsed and *frozen* by her dignity. These lines end thus:

> And ere the last collected shape he saw
> Of Artemis, dispersing fast amid
> Dense vapory clouds, the aching wintriness
> Had risen to his teeth, and fixed his eyes,
> Like glistening stones in the congealing air.

We refer, especially, too, to the description of *Love*, at page 29[36]; to that of a Bacchanalian orgie, at page 34[41]; to that of drought succeeded by rain, at page 70[37]; and to that of the palace of Eos, at page 104[92].

Mr. Horne has a very peculiar and very delightful faculty of enforcing, or giving vitality to a picture, by some one vivid and intensely characteristic point or touch. He seizes the most salient feature of his theme, and makes this feature convey the whole. The combined *näiveté* and picturesqueness of some of the passages thus enforced, cannot be sufficiently admired. For example:

> The arches soon
> *With bow-arm forward thrust*, on all sides twanged
> Around, above, below.

Now, it is this thrusting forward of the bow-arm which is the idiosyncrasy of the action of a mass of archers. Again: Rhexergon and his friends endeavor to persuade Akinetos to be king. Observe the silent refusal of Akinetos — the pecu-liar *passiveness* of his action — if we may be permitted the paradox.

> "Rise, therefore, Akinetos, thou art king."
> So saying, in his hand he placed a spear.
> *As though against a wall 'Twere set aslant,*
> *Flatly the long spear fell upon the ground.*

Here again: Merope departs from Chios in a ship.

> And, as it sped along, she closely pressed
> The rich globes of her bosom on the side
> O'er which she bent with those black eyes, and gazed
> Into the sea *that fled beneath her face.*

The fleeing of the sea beneath the face of one who gazes into it from a ship's side, is the idiosyncrasy of the action of the subject. It is that which chiefly impresses the gazer.

We conclude with some brief quotations at random, which we shall not pause to classify. Their merits need no demonstration. They *gleam* with the purest imagination. They abound in picturesqueness — force — happily chosen epithets, each in itself a picture. They are redolent of all for which a poet will value a poem.

> —her silver sandals glanced i' the rays,
> As doth a lizard playing on a hill,
> And on the spot where she that instant stood
> Naught but the bent and quivering grass was seen.

> Above the Isle of Chios, night by night,
> The clear moon lingered ever on her course,
> Covering the forest foliage, where it swept
> In its unbroken breadth along the slopes,
> With placid silver; edging leaf and trunk
> Where gloom clung deep around; but chiefly sought
> *With melancholy splendor to illume*
> *The dark-mouthed caverns where Orion lay,*
> *Dreaming among his kinsmen.*

> The ocean realm below, and all its caves
> And bristling vegetation, plant and flower,
> And forests in their dense petrific shade
> *Where the tides moan for sleep that never comes.*

> A fawn, who on a quiet green knoll sat
> Somewhat apart, sang a melodious ode,
> *Made rich by harmonies of hidden strings.*
> Autarces seized a satyr, with intent,
> Despite his writhing freaks and furious face,
> To dash him on a gong, but that amidst

The struggling mass Encolyon thrust a pine,
Heavy and black as Charon's ferrying pole,
O'er which they, *like a bursting billow*, fell.

—then round the blaze,
Their shadows brandishing afar and athwart,
Over the level space and up the hills,
Six giants held portentous dance.

—his safe return
To corporal sense, by shaking off these nets
Of moonbeams from his soul.

—old memories
Slumbrously hung above the purple line
Of distance, to the East, while odorously
Glistened the tear-drops of a new-fall'n shower.

Sing on!
Sing on, great tempest! in the darkness sing!
Thy madness is a music that brings calm
Into my central soul; and from its waves,
That now with joy begin to heave and gush,
The burning image of all life's desire,
Like an absorbing, fire-breathed, phantom god,
Rises and floats! here touching on the foam,
There hovering over it; *ascending swift
Starward, then swooping down the hemisphere
Upon the lengthening javelins of the blast!*

Now a sound we heard,
Like to some well-known voice in prayer; and next
An iron clang *that* seemed to break great bonds
Beneath the earth, shook us to conscious life.
It is Oblivion! In his hand — though naught
Knows he of this — a dusky purple flower
Droops over its tall stem. Again! ah see!
He wanders into mist and now is lost! —
Within his brain what lovely realms of death
Are pictured, and what knowledge through the doors
Of his forgetfulness of all the earth
A path may gain?

But we are positively forced to conclude. It was our design to give "Orion" a careful and methodical analysis — thus to bring clearly forth its multitudinous beauties to the eye of the American public. Our limits have constrained us to treat it in an imperfect and cursory manner. We have had to content ourselves chiefly with assertion, where our original purpose was to demonstrate. We have left unsaid a hundred things which a well-grounded enthusiasm would have prompted us to say. One thing, however, we must and will say, in conclusion. "Orion" will be admitted, by every man of genius, to be one of the noblest, if not the very noblest poetical work of the age. Its defects are trivial and conventional — its beauties intrinsic and *supreme*.

www.ingramcontent.com/pod-product-compliance
Lightning Source LLC
Chambersburg PA
CBHW030105240426
43661CB00001B/16